OREGON WILDLIFE VIEWING GUIDE

James A. Yuskavitch

FALCON™

Falcon Press® Publishing Co., Inc.,
Helena, Montana

ACKNOWLEDGEMENTS

Many people contributed their time and expertise to bring this project to a successful completion. First and foremost, I would like to thank the following agencies that provided the funding to make this book possible: the U.S. Fish and Wildlife Service, Bureau of Land Management, Department of Defense, U.S. Forest Service, National Fish and Wildlife Foundation, Oregon Parks and Recreation Department, and the Oregon Department of Fish and Wildlife.

The members of the steering committee provided invaluable advice, direction, information, and expertise in selecting viewing sites and developing interpretive materials. Steering committee members included Lisa Norris, Don Virgovic, and Jim Pollock of the U.S. Forest Service; Erick Campbell and Ken White of the Bureau of Land Management; Dick Kuehner and Sheila McCarten of the U.S. Fish and Wildlife Service; Monte Turner and Margie Willis of the Oregon Parks and Recreation Department; and Shann Weston of the Oregon Department of Fish and Wildlife.

I would also like to express my appreciation to Kate Davies, Sara Vickerman, and Wendy Hudson of Defenders of Wildlife, and John Grassy of Falcon Press for their assistance, advice, and moral support throughout the project. Roy Lowe of the U.S. Fish and Wildlife Service provided invaluable assistance with coastal viewing sites. The Nature Conservancy's Natural Heritage Program provided technical information on Oregon's physiographic provinces. Special thanks to Reed Noss for reviewing interpretive text.

Last but not least, nearly one hundred people, field staff and site managers, provided information on their respective viewing sites and reviewed the text for accuracy. Thank you one and all.

Author and State Project Manager
James A. Yuskavitch

National Watchable Wildlife Program Manager
Kate Davies, Defenders of Wildlife

Illustrator
Jerry Werner

Front cover photo
Bobcat   DENVER BRYAN

Back cover photos
Tanner Creek, Columbia Gorge NSA   GERRY ELLIS
Trumpeter Swan with cygnets   ART WOLFE

CONTENTS

Copyright © 1994 by Falcon Press Publishing Co., Inc.,
Helena and Billings, Montana. Illustrations copyright © 1994
by Defenders of Wildlife, Washington, D.C.
Published in cooperation with Defenders of Wildlife.

Defenders of Wildlife and its design are registered
marks of Defenders of Wildlife, Washington, D.C.

Design, typesetting, and other prepress work by Falcon Press, Helena, Montana.

Printed in the United States of America.

Cataloging-in-Publication Data

Yuskavitch, James.
    Oregon wildlife viewing guide / James Yuskavitch.
        p. cm. -- (The Watchable wildlife series)
    Includes index.
    ISBN 1-56044-271-9
    1. Wildlife viewing sites--Oregon--Guidebooks. 2. Wildlife
watching--Oregon--Guidebooks. I. Title. II. Series.
    QL201.Y87 1994   93-46140
    596.09795--dc20   CIP

PROJECT SPONSORS

 DEFENDERS OF WILDLIFE is a national nonprofit organization of more than 80,000 members dedicated to preserving the natural abundance and diversity of wildlife and its habitat. A one-year membership is $20 and includes subscriptions to *Defenders*, an award-winning conservation magazine, and *Wildlife Advocate*, an activist-oriented newsletter. To join, or for further information, write or call Defenders of Wildlife, 1101 14th St. NW, Suite 1400, Washington, DC 20005, (202) 682-9400.

 The U.S. FISH AND WILDLIFE SERVICE administers nearly 575,000 acres of land and water in Oregon. The mission of the U.S. Fish and Wildlife Service is to conserve, protect, and enhance fish and wildlife and their habitats for the continuing benefit of the American people. Programs include the National Wildlife Refuge System, protection of threatened and endangered species, conservation of migratory birds, fisheries restoration, recreation/education, wildlife research, and law enforcement. U.S. Fish and Wildlife Service, 911 NE 11th Avenue, Portland, OR 97232, (503) 231-6828.

 The BUREAU OF LAND MANAGEMENT cares for nearly 16 million acres in Oregon. As the nation's largest conservation agency, the Bureau of Land Management is dedicated to providing quality habitat to ensure a natural abundance of fish, wildlife, and plants on public lands. The Bureau of Land Management manages the many resources on the public lands—minerals, range, cultural sites, wild horses and burrows, wilderness, recreation, and more—under the principles of multiuse and sustained yield, and within the framework of environmental responsibility. Bureau of Land Management, 1300 NE 44th Avenue, Portland, OR 97213, (503) 280-7002.

 The FOREST SERVICE, U.S. DEPARTMENT OF AGRICULTURE, has a mandate to protect, improve, and wisely use the nation's forest and range resources for multiple purposes to benefit all Americans. Oregon's national forests containing 15,631,961 acres, are sponsors of this program to promote awareness and enjoyment of fish and wildlife on our national forest lands. For more information, contact USFS, 333 SW 1st Avenue, Portland, OR 97204, (503) 326-2971.

The DEPARTMENT OF DEFENSE is the steward of about 25 million acres of land in the United States, many of which possess irreplaceable natural and cultural resources. The DOD is pleased to support the Watchable Wildlife program through its Legacy Resource Management Program, a special initiative to enhance the conservation and restoration of natural and cultural resources on military land. For more information, contact the Office of the Deputy Under Secretary of Defense (Environmental Security), 400 Army Navy Drive, Suite 206, Arlington, VA 22202-2884.

THE NATIONAL FISH AND WILDLIFE FOUNDATION, chartered by Congress to stimulate private giving to conservation, is an independent nonprofit organization. Using federally-funded challenge grants, it forges partnerships between the public and private sectors to conserve the nation's fish, wildlife, and plants. National Fish and Wildlife Foundation, Bender Bldg., Suite 900, 1120 Connecticut Avenue, NW, Washington, DC 20036. (202) 857-0166.

THE OREGON PARKS AND RECREATION DEPARTMENT is responsible for more than 90,000 acres of natural and recreational resources. Much of this acreage provides habitat for a great abundance and diversity of wildlife. Department efforts to provide recreational access to wildlife populations while preserving their ecosystems are guided by popular demand and its mission: "Provide and protect outstanding natural, scenic, cultural, historic, and recreation sites for the enjoyment and education of present and future generations." Opportunities for wildlife viewing have been enhanced at many parks. For more information, contact Oregon Parks and Recreation Department, 1115 Commercial Street N.E., Salem, OR 97310, or call (503) 378-6305.

THE OREGON DEPARTMENT OF FISH AND WILDLIFE is dedicated to protecting and enhancing Oregon's fish and wildlife and their habitats for the use and enjoyment by present and future generations. Oregon Department of Fish and Wildlife, 2501 SW 1st Avenue, Portland, OR 97201 (503) 229-5410.

INTRODUCTION

From rocky coast and lush coniferous forest to spectacular mountains and bone-dry desert, Oregon offers a dazzling array of wildlife watching opportunities. You do not need lots of specialized equipment to enjoy this fast-growing pastime. A pair of binoculars and a few field guides will do it. Nor does watching wildlife require expertise in natural history. All that's needed is an interest in Oregon's diverse wildlife.

Pursue wildlife watching as casually or as seriously as suits your fancy. Drive the coastline and watch whales from a roadside turnout, strike off into remote backcountry on foot in search of bighorn sheep, or experience some of the many other opportunities in between these extremes. Pick a site close to home and get to know its wildlife throughout the seasons, or journey across the state to places you have never been before. The choice is yours. Oregon's wildlife country beckons you to go exploring, to meet its inhabitants.

THE NATIONAL WATCHABLE WILDLIFE PROGRAM

Many of Oregon's wildlife areas were purchased with funding provided by sportsmen through license fees and taxes on hunting and fishing equipment. This has enabled state and federal agencies to acquire important wildlife habitat such as wetlands for waterfowl and winter feeding ranges for elk, deer, and pronghorn. Non-game wildlife species have benefitted as well from these habitat acquisition efforts.

Today, hunting revenues are decreasing, providing less money for habitat protection, while threats to wildlife and their habitats continue to grow. At the same time, many people across the country are becoming interested in viewing wildlife in a natural environment. The Oregon Watchable Wildlife Project is part of a national effort to encourage wildlife viewing, and, of particular importance, to develop new sources of funding for wildlife habitat protection programs. Government agencies and private organizations are joining forces throughout the state to promote wildlife viewing in Oregon.

This guide represents only part of the National Watchable Wildlife Program. This program, coordinated by Defenders of Wildlife, is establishing a network of wildlife viewing sites throughout the nation, and wildlife viewing guides are being produced for every state. Look for the binocular logo watchable wildlife signs as you travel in Oregon, and in other states, directing you to nearby wildlife viewing areas.

Finally, as you visit the sites described in this guide and enjoy viewing Oregon's wildlife, remember that they require your concern and support if they are to continue to have a place in our future.

VIEWING HINTS

This guide is designed to help you see wildlife by describing where to go, when to go, and where to look once you get there. You probably will not see all the wildlife listed at a viewing area every time you visit. But following the viewing hints listed below will greatly increase your chances for seeing the maximum amount of wildlife.

Dawn and dusk are the times of highest wildlife activity. Areas that are barren of wildlife at midday may have been teeming with various kinds of animals during the early morning hours. Those who arrive early and stay late see more wildlife.

Visit viewing sites during the appropriate seasons. Many species of wildlife appear only during certain seasons at any given site. They may hibernate for the winter, roam from habitat to habitat as the seasons change, or migrate through at particular times of the year. Check site listings in this guide for the best times to visit each site.

Use field guides. Many good field guides are available to help identify mammals, birds, reptiles, amphibians, and other flora and fauna. Knowing more about the wildlife will greatly enhance your viewing pleasure.

Use binoculars and spotting scopes. Wild animals are generally wary of humans and keep their distance. Binoculars and spotting scopes allow much better views of most wildlife.

Patience is a virtue. Expect to spend some time at a particular place, or return several times, before you see wildlife, especially if looking for a particular species.

Use Blinds. Some viewing areas have blinds available to the public. Using them will help you get closer to wildlife. In more popular areas, wildlife often become accustomed to vehicles. It is often possible to approach them more closely by staying in your vehicle.

Ask an expert. Some viewing areas have on-site staff. Do not be afraid to ask them for advice. They often have the most up-to-date viewing information on their site.

Do not disturb or feed the wildlife. Keep a respectful distance—you are too close if the animal changes its behavior because of your presence. Be especially careful around nesting areas. Causing animals to run or fly, particularly during winter, forces them to unnecessarily expend energy. Feeding animals only makes them dependant on humans, decreasing their odds for survival.

Wildlife can be dangerous. Elk and deer can cause injury with the kick of a sharp hoof. The bite of a small animal, even a chipmunk, can cause infection or disease. For the sake of you and the wildlife, keep your distance.

HOW TO USE THIS GUIDE

This guide is organized into seven sections, roughly coinciding with the various ecological regions of the state. Each site entry describes the general habitat of the area, the wildlife visitors are most likely to see, suggestions on the best times to visit, and the best places for viewing within each area. Each listing also gives directions to the site, area ownership, and an information phone number. **Note: Always travel with an up-to-date road map.** Also included are the site's size and the closest town with facilities. Accompanying symbols provide a quick reference to each site's featured wildlife and facilities. *NOTES OF CAUTION PERTAINING TO SAFETY, ROAD CONDITIONS, OR OTHER RESTRICTIONS APPEAR IN CAPITAL LETTERS.*

FEATURED WILDLIFE

Songbirds Perching Birds	Waterfowl	Upland Birds	Wading Birds
Birds of Prey	Marine Birds	Shorebirds	Bats
Hoofed Mammals	Carnivores Mammals	Small Mammals	Freshwater Mammals
Reptiles, Amphibians	Tidepools	Seals, Sea Lions, Otters	Whales, Dolphins
Fish	Wildflowers		

FACILITIES AND RECREATION

Parking	Restrooms	Picnic	Campground
Trails	Handicapped Access	Entry Fee	Restaurant
Lodging	Boat Ramp	Large boats	Small Boats

SITE OWNER/MANAGER ABBREVIATIONS

USFWS	U.S. Fish and Wildlife Service	NPS	National Park Service
BLM	Bureau of Land Mngt.	OPRD	Oregon Parks and Recreation Department
ACE	U.S. Army Corps of Engineers	ODFW	Oregon Department of Fish and Wildlife
USFS	U.S. Forest Service	DSL	Division of State Lands
DOD	Department of Defense	PVT	Private

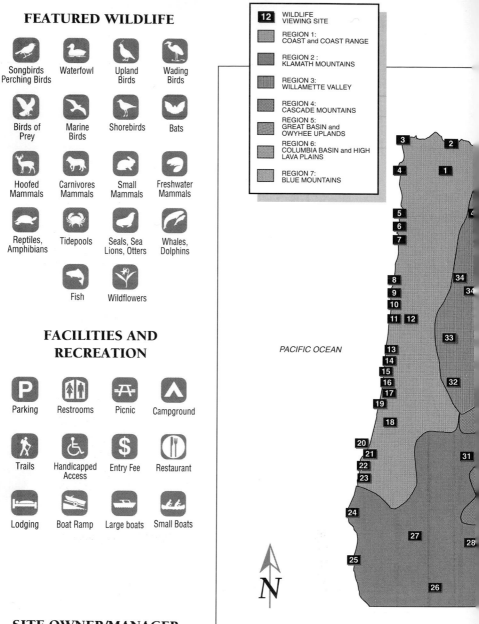

12 WILDLIFE VIEWING SITE

REGION 1: COAST and COAST RANGE

REGION 2: KLAMATH MOUNTAINS

REGION 3: WILLAMETTE VALLEY

REGION 4: CASCADE MOUNTAINS

REGION 5: GREAT BASIN and OWYHEE UPLANDS

REGION 6: COLUMBIA BASIN and HIGH LAVA PLAINS

REGION 7: BLUE MOUNTAINS

PACIFIC OCEAN

N

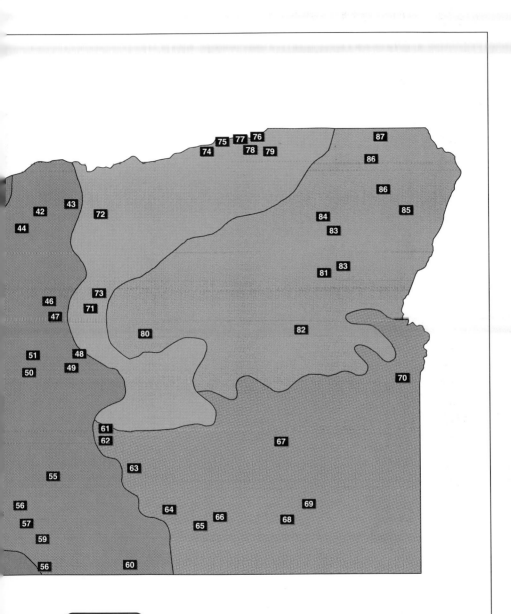

HIGHWAY SIGNS

As you travel in Oregon and other states, look for these signs on highways and other roads. They identify the route to follow to reach wildlife viewing sites.

REGION 1: COAST and COAST RANGE

Rocky coast, headlands jutting into the ocean, sandy beaches, dunes, life-rich estuaries and a mountain range cloaked in Douglas-fir and western hemlock intersected by a coastal strip of spruce and hemlock forest marks this diverse region, where sea meets land. Here, black bears roam in sight of great whales spouting and breaching offshore while Pacific salmon move between open ocean and inland rivers according to their seasons and cycles.

Photo, opposite page: Crescent and Cannon beaches, northern coast.
LARRY GEDDIS

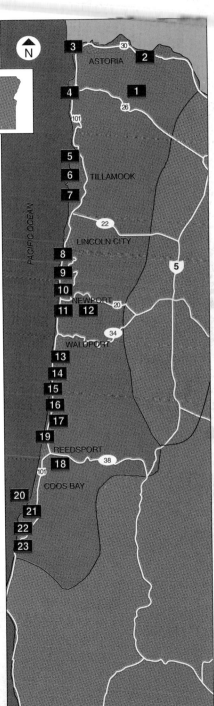

Wildlife Viewing Sites

1   Jewell Meadows Wildlife Area
2   Lewis and Clark National Wildlife Refuge
3   Fort Stevens State Park
4   Ecola State Park and Haystack Rock
5   Bayocean Peninsula
6   Cape Meares State Park and National Wildlife Refuge and Three Arch Rocks National Wildlife Refuge
7   Cape Lookout State Park and Netarts Bay
8   Siletz Bay Park
9   Boiler Bay, Rocky Creek and Otter Crest State Waysides
10   Yaquina Head Outstanding Natural Area
11   Mark O. Hatfield Marine Science Center
12   Oregon Coast Aquarium
13   Yachats Ocean Road State Wayside
14   Cape Perpetua Visitors Center
15   Strawberry Hill in Neptune State Park
16   Devil's Elbow State Park and Oregon Islands National Wildlife Refuge
17   Sea Lion Caves
18   Dean Creek Elk Viewing Area
19   Oregon Dunes National Recreation Area
20   Cape Arago, Sunset Bay, Shore Acres State Parks and Oregon Islands National Wildlife Refuge
21   South Slough National Estuarine Research Reserve
22   Bullards Beach State Park and Bandon Marsh National Wildlife Refuge
23   New River

1 JEWELL MEADOWS WILDLIFE AREA

Description: Although known primarily for its population of Roosevelt elk, the diverse habitats found at this site provide a home to a variety of wildlife. Coniferous and deciduous forest, meadows, small ponds and streams, abandoned orchards, and sedge wetlands are home to black-tailed deer and coyote, birds of prey, and numerous songbirds.

Viewing Information: A herd of 75 to 200 elk roam this area and can be seen almost daily, between September and March, feeding and resting in meadows along Fishhawk and Beneke creeks. The best viewing begins in November when elk are out in number throughout the day. Area staff take visitors out to feed the elk on a daily basis from December through March 15. Call ahead for further information. Excellent winter viewing of songbirds and red-tailed hawks; bald eagles occasionally seen. Elk are less conspicuous during summer, but may be seen in early morning or late afternoon.

Directions: From Portland, take U.S. Highway 26 west about 50 miles to Jewell Junction. Turn north on the unmarked state highway and drive 9 miles to Jewell. The site is located 1.5 miles west of Jewell on Oregon Highway 202.

Ownership: ODFW (503) 755-2264
Size: 1,150 acres **Closest Town:** Astoria

2 LEWIS AND CLARK NATIONAL WILDLIFE REFUGE

Description: Some 20 islands dot this refuge of sandbars, tidal marshes, and mudflats in the estuary of the Columbia River. Stretching for 15 miles, this is the largest marsh in western Oregon and an important stopover for migrating waterfowl. Watch for redhead, canvasback, scaup, mallard, goldeneye, and bufflehead. Geese include Canada, snow, and white-fronted species; tundra swans winter here. Osprey and bald eagle are also common. Best viewing is by boat. Canoes are particularly useful for navigating channels. *BOATERS AND CANOEIST SHOULD BEWARE OF TIDAL FLUCTUATIONS AND CHANGING WEATHER CONDITIONS. AVOID THE SHIPPING CHANNEL.*

Viewing Information: Ducks are best seen October through January. Look for geese from September through March, and swans December through March. Bald eagle concentrations peak during winter, but are also readily seen during spring nesting. Osprey are most often seen April through August.

Directions: Drive 9 miles west of Westport on U.S. Highway 30. Follow signs north to Brownsmead and Aldrich Point, which has a boat ramp.

Ownership: USFWS (206) 795-3915
Size: 35,000 acres **Closest Town:** Knappa

3 FORT STEVENS STATE PARK

Description: The rich variety of wildlife habitat offered by this coastal park includes coniferous forest, scrublands, sandy and grassy beaches, estuary, mudflats, saltwater marsh, freshwater swamp, and lakes. Deer, elk, beaver, and many kinds of waterfowl, shorebirds, wading birds, and songbirds can be seen here. Whale watching programs are offered in December and March.

Viewing Information: Fall, winter, and spring are best. Look for great blue heron, mallard, wood duck, and beaver at Coffenbury Lake. A two-mile hiking trail loops around the lake. At South Jetty Overlook watch for harbor seal and gray whale, and cormorant, western grebe, auklet, and various species of gulls on the water. Bald eagle, long-billed dowitcher, great blue heron, various wren species, robin, and northern harrier may be seen at the Trestle Bay viewing blind. Swash Lake viewing blind is a good place to see Roosevelt elk, black-tailed deer, beaver, wood duck, mallard, and Virginia rail.

Directions: *From Astoria, go 2 miles west on U.S. Highway 101. Turn right at Warrenton Junction and follow signs to park.*

Ownership: OPRD (503) 861-3170
Size: 3,700 acres   **Closest Town:** Astoria

4 ECOLA STATE PARK AND HAYSTACK ROCK

Description: Rugged headlands, high cliffs, broad ocean views, and tidepools offer a variety of wildlife viewing here. Marine birds to watch for include tufted puffin, common murre, cormorant, and numerous gulls. Mammals include harbor seal, California and Steller sea lion, and gray whale. Haystack Rock is part of the Oregon Islands National Wildlife Refuge. *COLLECTING TIDEPOOL SPECIMENS AND TRESPASS ON THE ROCK ARE PROHIBITED.*

Viewing Information: Winter and spring offer best viewing. Look for cormorants, murres, and puffins on offshore rocks and rocky headlands. Seals and sea lions bask on rocks. Whales are best seen March through May from headlands. Look for tufted puffins at Haystack Rock April through September. Cormorants and murres nest in large numbers on Bird Rocks at Chapman Point beginning in April. View Haystack Rock from adjacent beach.

Directions: *Haystack Rock is located off U.S. Highway 101 at the south end of Cannon Beach. Ecola State Park is 3 miles north of Cannon Beach on U.S. 101.*

Ownership: OPRD, USFWS (503) 861-1671, 867-4550
Size: 1,304 acres; 5 acres   **Closest Town:** Cannon Beach

15

5 BAYOCEAN PENINSULA

Description: Jutting out from Cape Meares into Tillamook Bay, Bayocean Peninsula offers a mix of pine/spruce forest, grassy dunes, sandy beach, wetlands, and mudflats. Look for the tracks of black-tailed deer and raccoon in the sand and mud. Gray whales pass offshore in spring and fall, and orcas sometimes stray into the bay to hunt harbor seals.

Viewing Information: Shorebirds are most numerous during spring and fall. Brown pelican, bald eagle, and great blue heron are seen spring, summer, and fall. Watch for Caspian terns diving for fish in the bay during these seasons. In June, beach walkers may find seal pups hauled-out on the sand. Leave them alone, as the mother has just temporarily "parked" them there while she hunts for food. Whales are most likely to be seen on the ocean side of the peninsula in November, December, March, and April.

Directions: Take Netarts Highway west from Tillamook to Bayocean Road. Follow Bayocean Road to peninsula.

Ownership: Tillamook County, Pvt. (503) 322-3477
Size: 1,200 acres   **Closest Town:** Tillamook

6 CAPE MEARES STATE PARK AND NATIONAL WILDLIFE REFUGE, THREE ARCH ROCKS NATIONAL WILDLIFE REFUGE

Description: Steep cliffs and an old-growth forest of western hemlock and Sitka spruce characterize this state park and adjacent wildlife refuge. The cliffs and offshore islands provide nesting habitat for the common murre, pelagic cormorant, pigeon guillemot, and tufted puffin. Harbor seal, California sea lion, and gray whale are also seen here. A trail runs between the park and refuge. Nearby Three Arch Rocks National Wildlife Refuge hosts 250,000 nesting seabirds each year, particularly common murres. Storm petrel, cormorant, gulls, pigeon guillemot, and puffin also nest here. Steller sea lions haul-out and pup here.

Viewing Information: Seabirds nest from April through August. Gray whales can be seen from headlands December through January and March through May. Seals and sea lions haul-out on the lower portions of offshore rocks year-round. Bald eagles are sometimes seen in the area. A spotting scope is highly recommended for observing birds on offshore rocks.

Directions: Cape Meares is 9 miles west of Tillamook on the Three Capes Scenic Route. Three Arch Rocks National Wildlife Refuge is best observed from Oceanside State Park, 2 miles south of Cape Meares on Three Capes Scenic Route.

Ownership: OPRD, USFWS (503) 842-4981, 867-4550
Size: 233 acres; 17 acres   **Closest Town:** Tillamook

Description: A 2.3-mile trail leads through a mature forest of Sitka spruce-western hemlock to the tip of Cape Lookout and expansive views of the ocean and Netarts Bay. More than 150 species of birds have been recorded here. Seabirds are especially numerous, including pigeon guillemot, common murre, pelagic cormorant, auklet, western gull, tufted puffin, brown pelican, and sanderling. Cape Lookout is an outstanding place to watch for gray whales. A quarter-mile nature trail offers a closer look at local flora.

Viewing Information: April through July is best for seabirds. Gray whales migrate off the coast in November, December and March. Harbor seals can be seen year-round basking on offshore rocks. Large flocks of sanderlings, dowitchers, dunlins, and sandpipers gather on Netarts Bay in spring and fall. Brown pelicans and an occasional peregrine falcon are seen during summer. Brant and Aleutian Canada geese winter on the bay. Watch for bald eagle and great blue heron year-round.

Directions: *Cape Lookout State Park is located 11 miles southwest of Tillamook on the Three Capes Scenic Route. Netarts Bay can be viewed from Cape Lookout, or accessed from the town of Netarts, on the north shore of the bay.*

Ownership: OPRD, Tillamook County (503) 842-4981, 322-3477
Size: 2,000 acres, 2,325 acres   **Closest Town:** Tillamook

Pigeon guillemots belong to a family of seabirds whose legs are set back on their bodies, an adaptation for swimming and diving. On land, their upright stance earns them the nickname, "penguin of the north." During the nesting season they are readily observed, along with other seabirds, on rocky headlands and offshore rocks.

ART WOLFE

8 SILETZ BAY PARK

Description: Sandy beach, intertidal estuary, and creek provide opportunities for viewing harbor seal, great blue heron, belted kingfisher, brown pelican, loon, red-necked and horned grebe, western sandpiper, dunlin, bald eagle, barn and violet-green swallow, whimbrel, and a variety of waterfowl.

Viewing Information: Look for seals year-round. Brown pelican, tern, whimbrel, heron, and kingfisher are common in summer. Western sandpiper, dunlin, and other shorebirds gather at high tide. Bald eagle, loon, and grebes are seen in winter. The bay is also accessible from the Taft Dock on the east end of 51st Street. Viewing telescopes are available here and at the park. Hershey's Place, a local restaurant, also has viewing telescopes. Salishan Lodge has a trail for guests. The estuary is also easily viewed from the highway.

Directions: The park is in Lincoln City on U.S. Highway 101, just north of Schooner Creek. Hershey's Place is on the north end of the bay, and Salishan Lodge, on the south end, off of U.S. 101.

Ownership: City of Lincoln City (503) 994-2131
Size: 1 acre   **Closest Town:** Lincoln City

9 BOILER BAY, ROCKY CREEK, AND OTTER CREST STATE WAYSIDES

Description: Three roadside overlooks offer panoramic views of the ocean and good birding for the many seabird species that live along the coast.

Viewing Information: Birding is best from March through November. At Boiler Bay look for black-footed albatross, Murphy's and storm petrel, horned puffin, Clark's grebe, black-vented shearwater, and other rare visitors to the Oregon coast, particularly after a storm. Black oystercatchers nest at Rocky Creek and Boiler Bay. Brown pelicans are common during summer, and bald eagle are regularly seen here. Pelagic cormorant, tufted puffin, and pigeon guillemot nest on rocky headlands at Otter Crest.

Directions: All three waysides are on U.S. Highway 101. Boiler Bay is 0.5 mile north of Depoe Bay. Rocky Creek is 1 mile south of Depoe Bay and Otter Crest is 2.5 miles further south.

Ownership: OPRD (503) 265-4560
Size: 32.8 acres; 58.4 acres; 1.5 acres   **Closest Town:** Depoe Bay

Description: This rugged headland jutting into the Pacific Ocean provides some of the best wildlife viewing on the coast. Headlands and adjacent rocks harbor a variety of colonial nesting birds, including the common murre, cormorant, tufted puffin, pigeon guillemot, and various species of gull. Harbor seals and California sea lions bob in the surf, or haul-out on rocks to sunbathe. Migrating gray whales pass by just offshore. The historic Yaquina Head Lighthouse, built in 1872, rises from the headland. Stairs lead down the south side of the headland to a beach and tidepools.

Viewing Information: Sea birds are most common from March through August. Look for them on rocky outcrops or flying along the shore. Brown pelicans are in the area from June to September. Look for seals and sea lions sunning on offshore rocks or swimming in the waves year-round. Gray whales can be seen from March through May as they migrate to their Alaskan feeding grounds. The best viewing conditions are during early morning on calm, overcast days. Scan the water's surface for blows—plumes of water or vapor. Lucky visitors may see whales jumping or breaching. Careful exploration of the tidepools at low tide reveals hermit crabs, sea urchins, anemones, barnacles, sea stars, and small fish stranded by the receding water. *ALWAYS USE EXTREME CAUTION WHEN WANDERING ALONG THE OCEAN. ROCKS CAN BE SLIPPERY. LARGE, UNEXPECTED WAVES CAN KNOCK PEOPLE DOWN AND SEND HEAVY DRIFTWOOD FLYING.*

Directions: *From Newport drive north 3.4 miles on U.S. Highway 101. Turn west onto Lighthouse Drive and follow signs to headland and lighthouse.*

Ownership: BLM (503) 867-4851
Size: 100 acres   **Closest Town:** Newport

Low tide provides exciting wildlife viewing, when sea stars, barnacles, hermit crabs, small fish, and perhaps even an octopus or jellyfish are temporarily exposed in tidepools and on rocks. Since the animals are very vulnerable at this time, be careful not to disturb them. GARY BRAASCH

11 MARK O. HATFIELD MARINE SCIENCE CENTER

Description: The center features aquarium exhibits, natural history displays, films, guided tours, educational programs, and whale-watching interpretive programs. A one-mile nature trail leads visitors through lupine and beachgrass and along adjacent estuary channel and mudflats. A variety of birds can be viewed along the trail, including bufflehead, double-crested cormorant, horned grebe, pigeon guillemot, common loon, red-breasted merganser, brown pelican, and surf and white-winged scoter. Also watch for northern harrier, American crow, western gull, Caspian tern, song sparrow, and barn swallow. Less often seen are California ground squirrel, garter snake, and northern alligator lizard.

Viewing Information: From the nature trail, scan the open water for cormorants, scoters, mergansers, loons, and other diving birds. Fall and winter are the best seasons for viewing American wigeon and other ducks and geese. Scaup may be seen diving in the estuary from September through May. Shorebirds are best seen in spring and fall. At low tide watch for whimbrel, dunlin, and sandpipers on mudflats as they probe for food. Brown pelicans fish here during summer and fall. Painted lady and swallowtail butterflies, sand wasps, and dragonflies are in the air during summer. Harbor seals are sometimes seen in the open water; or look for them at nearby South Jetty.

Directions: *In Newport, off of U.S. Highway 101 on Marine Science Drive, just south of the Yaquina Bay Bridge. Follow signs. To reach South Jetty, go west underneath the bridge and follow road to jetty.*

Ownership: Oregon State University (503) 867-0100
Size: 2 acres   **Closest Town:** Newport

The Oregon Coast Aquarium features indoor and outdoor exhibits introducing visitors to the rich diversity of Oregon's coastal environment. Sea otters, seals, sea lions, and a variety of seabirds are just a sampling of the creatures that may be observed in carefully-detailed recreations of natural environments.
GARY BRAASCH

12 OREGON COAST AQUARIUM

Description: This facility on the estuary of Yaquina Bay offers first-rate exhibits and displays of coastal habitats, including dunes, deep rocky pools, caves, cliffs, and tidepools. Also on display, in natural settings, are a variety of coastal invertebrates and fish, along with tufted puffin, pigeon guillemot, rhinoceros auklet, common murre, harbor seal, and sea lion. This is the only place in Oregon to view sea otters.

Viewing Information: Exhibits are available indoors and outdoors. Inside exhibits include sandy shores, rocky shores, coastal waters, whale theater, wetlands, and interactive displays. Wildlife exhibits outside include the seabird aviary, seals and sea lions, sea otters, Pacific octopus, and tidepool inhabitants.

Directions: *In Newport off of U.S. Highway 101 on Ferry Slip Road, just south of the Yaquina Bay Bridge.*

Ownership: Private (503) 867-3123
Size: 32 acres   **Closest Town:** Newport

13 YACHATS OCEAN ROAD STATE WAYSIDE

Description: The Yachats River flows into a small bay at the town of Yachats, where the heavily forested mountains of the Coast Range rise immediately above the shoreline. This is an excellent area to view a variety of gulls, including western, glaucous-winged, mew, California, and ring-billed species. Other shorebirds are common.

Viewing Information: Park at Yachats Ocean Road State Wayside and walk down trail to beach or view from Wayside. Fall through spring are the best times to observe birds here. Look for gulls on the beach at the mouth of the river. Other birds, including the common loon, black turnstone, wandering tattler, scoter, and grebe, may be seen on the rocks and in the surf.

Directions: *To reach the viewing area, go south from Yachats on U.S. Highway 101. Turn right immediately after crossing Yachats River bridge onto Yachats Ocean Wayside Road. Parking areas and trails to the beach are on right.*

Ownership: OPRD (503) 867-7451
Size: 79 acres   **Closest Town:** Yachats

OREGON BIODIVERSITY:
THE LIFE CYCLE OF THE SALMON

Born in inland streams, growing to adulthood in the ocean, and returning to their natal rivers to spawn and die, Pacific salmon exemplify the cycles of nature and the rebirth that springs from death.

Salmon are important to nature's economy. They not only provide food for a variety of other animals, but their decomposing bodies effectively recycle nutrients from the sea back to the forests of their birth.

Salmon are equally important to the human economy, in the form of sport and commercial fishing. The culture of Pacific Northwest Native Americans evolved around the salmon, providing them with physical and spiritual sustenance.

Coho salmon, pictured here, along with Chinook, pink, and chum salmon, are all found in Oregon. Overharvesting, habitat destruction, and excessive planting of hatchery fish all pose a continuing threat to these majestic wild creatures.

14 CAPE PERPETUA VISITOR CENTER

Description: This densely forested headland rises 803 feet above the booming surf. A variety of coastal forest species live here including bobcat, cougar, and black bear. Birds include great horned, spotted, and pygmy owl, bald eagle, dark-eyed junco, black-capped chickadee, and rufous-sided towhee. Marbled murrelets bob in the waves. Numerous tidepools dot the rocky shoreline. The visitor center offers natural history and historical exhibits, a hiking trail, and a nearby 22-mile driving tour.

Viewing Information: Walk the trail from the visitor center to the shore. Watch for forest songbirds and chipmunks. The rufous hummingbird is seen here during early spring and summer. The cape offers excellent opportunities to explore tidepools. Look for sea stars, anemones, sea urchins, barnacles, and hermit crabs. Gray whales can be seen from the visitor center observation deck or from the overlook along U.S. Highway 101 in November and December, and February through March. *DO NOT DISTURB TIDEPOOL ANIMALS. BE ALERT FOR SLIPPERY ROCKS AND LARGE, UNEXPECTED WAVES.*

Directions: *From Yachats, go south 3 miles on U.S. Highway 101. Turn left at sign and follow road to visitor center.*

Ownership: USFS (503) 547-3289
Size: 2,700 acres **Closest Town:** Yachats

15 STRAWBERRY HILL IN NEPTUNE STATE PARK

Description: One hundred or more harbor seals may be seen basking on these near-shore rocks year-round. A turnout and parking area provide access. *IT IS A FEDERAL CRIME TO DISTURB MARINE MAMMALS. STAY AT LEAST 100 FEET AWAY FROM RESTING SEALS. MOVE AWAY SLOWLY IF YOUR APPROACH CAUSES THEM DISTRESS.*

Viewing Information: Although seals are commonly seen here throughout the year, larger concentrations occur during summer. Seals are present at any time of the day. Calm days and low tide provide the best viewing opportunities.

Directions: *On west side of U.S. Highway 101, 4 miles south of Yachats.*

Ownership: OPRD (503) 997-3851
Size: 4 acres **Closest Town:** Yachats

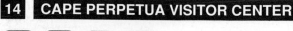

Description: These rocky bluffs and adjacent offshore rocks comprise a significant seabird nesting area. Double-crested and Brandt's cormorant, western gull, tufted puffin, and black oystercatcher are found here. Offshore rocks are part of the Oregon Islands National Wildlife Refuge. Heceta Head, with its picturesque lighthouse, overlooks the park and is a good place to watch for migrating gray whales.

Viewing Information: Spring and early summer are the best times to view seabirds as they congregate here to nest. Look for birds and their nests on the cliffs of offshore rocks. From Heceta Head, nesting seabirds can often be seen on the steep grassy slopes below the handrails. Look for white-winged and surf scoter in the water and black turnstone and wandering tattler on the rocks near the surf. Whales pass just offshore from March through May. Good opportunities to explore tidepools.

Directions: Go 12 miles north from Florence on U.S. Highway 101. The park is on the left just north of Cape Creek tunnel and bridge.

Ownership: OPRD, USFWS (503) 997-3851, 867-4550
Size: 547 acres   **Closest Town:** Florence

The harbor seal's habit of hauling up on rocks to bask in the sunshine makes this mammal easy to observe, if visitors know when and where to look. Capable of staying underwater for nearly half an hour, they feed as the tide comes in, then haul out onto offshore rocks during low tide. ART WOLFE

17 SEA LION CAVES

Description: California and Steller sea lions congregate here by the hundreds, in this largest sea cave in the U.S. Largest concentrations occur in fall and winter, particularly during stormy weather. Pigeon guillemot and rhinoceros auklet may also be seen in the cave during late spring and summer.

Viewing Information: Take the elevator to an outstanding viewpoint within the cave. An entry fee is charged.

Directions: On the west side of U.S. Highway 101, 12 miles north of Florence.

Ownership: Pvt. (503) 547-3111
Size: 99 acres   **Closest Town:** Florence

18 DEAN CREEK ELK VIEWING AREA

Description: A resident herd of 60 to 100 Roosevelt elk wander this mosaic of wetland, woodland, and meadow along the Umpqua River. Elk are easily viewed from turnouts along the highway; also watch for black-tailed deer. Birds to look for include Canada geese, mallard, osprey, western bluebird, and great blue heron. An interpretive center explains the local wildlife.

Viewing Information: Elk may be seen year-round. Early mornings and evenings are best. Park along the turnouts and scan the meadows, wetlands, and streamsides. When elk are lying down, look carefully for antlers rising above tall grass. Cows and newborn calves arrive in the meadows by mid-June. Bulls can be heard bugling during the mid-September to early-October breeding season. Deer are less common, but look for them along the forest edge behind the meadows. Ducks and herons may be seen in the wetlands.

Directions: 3 miles east of Reedsport on Oregon Highway 38 along the south side of the road.

Ownership: BLM, ODFW (503) 756-0100, 888-5515
Size: 1,040 acres   **Closest Town:** Reedsport

Description: Stretching for 40 miles along the ocean shore, this area encompasses a wide variety of coastal habitat ranging from coastal forest and grasslands to estuaries and salt marshes. More than 400 species of wildlife are found here including, California and Steller sea lion, harbor seal, mink, black-tailed deer, chickaree, and raccoon. Birds include double-crested cormorant, great blue heron, ruddy duck, northern harrier, blue grouse, Virginia rail, western sandpiper, and sanderling. The snowy plover, threatened with extinction, is also present.

Viewing Information: Siltcoos Lagoon is an old oxbow of the Siltcoos River, now a wetland and lake. It is an excellent place to see cinnamon teal, wood duck, great blue heron, American bittern, mallard, beaver, and black-tailed deer year-round. Another year-round viewing site is the Bluebill Lake Trail which leads through a 40-acre coastal wetland and meadow. Look for various species of warblers and woodpeckers. Dune beaches are good places to see migrating shorebirds in spring and fall. Sandy beaches also provide excellent opportunities to see tracks of black bear, bobcat, deer, skunk, and raccoon. In winter, sanderling, brown pelican, loon, and grebe gather in large numbers along beaches. Seals and sea lions are also seen. Large flocks of tundra swans gather in winter at South Jetty and can be viewed from the interpretive turnout. Numerous waterfowl and shorebirds assemble here during spring and fall migrations.

Directions: *Visit headquarters on U.S. Highway 101 in Reedsport, at north end of town. Obtain directions to above sites, as well as suggestions for others.*

Ownership: USFS (503) 271-3611
Size: 32,000 acres **Closest Town:** Reedsport

The Steller sea lion, named for its lion-like eyes and roar, may dive to 600 feet in search of fish, its primary prey. During their May through August mating season, bulls battle each other to defend their harems and territories. Large concentrations of sea lions may be observed basking on offshore rocks at many locations along the coast. ART WOLFE

20 CAPE ARAGO, SUNSET BAY, AND SHORE ACRES STATE PARKS AND OREGON ISLANDS NATIONAL WILDLIFE REFUGE

Description: Shell Island and Simpson Reef are the largest haul-out sites on the Oregon coast for California sea lions, northern elephant seals, and harbor seals. Steller sea lions and an occasional northern fur seal also rest here.

Viewing Information: View the offshore islands from various locations within the state parks. Seals and sea lions are present year-round. A spotting scope is recommended. The trail to North Cove is closed from March 1 to July 1 to protect seal pups. Gray whales may be seen passing by in winter and early spring.

Directions: From U.S. Highway 101 at Coos Bay, follow signs to Charleston and individual parks 14 miles south on the Cape Arago Highway.

Ownership: OPRD, USFWS (503) 888-4902, 867-4550
Size: 1,301 acres, 12 acres   **Closest Town:** Charleston

21 SOUTH SLOUGH NATIONAL ESTUARINE RESEARCH RESERVE

Description: This southern extension of the Coos Bay estuary was set aside for research and educational purposes under an agreement with the State of Oregon and the National Oceanic and Atmospheric Administration. Forested uplands, freshwater and saltmarshes, tideflats, and open channels all contribute to wildlife diversity. Watch for black-tailed deer, Roosevelt elk, raccoon, black bear, and brush rabbit. Birding is good for great blue heron, sanderling, sandpiper, dowitcher, killdeer, belted kingfisher, and numerous species of songbirds. An interpretive center is located on the reserve. Guided tours, self-guided trails, and workshops are available. Canoeing is permitted on the reserve's waterways.

Viewing Information: Spring, summer, and fall are the best times to visit. A popular hiking trail begins at the interpretive center, descends 300 feet through uplands, skunk cabbage swamp, and estuarine marsh, and ends at an observation platform overlooking the tideflats and the slough's open channel.

Directions: From U.S. Highway 101 at Coos Bay, follow signs to Charleston south via Cape Arago Highway. At Charleston, turn south onto Seven Devils Road. Interpretive center is 4 miles south of Charleston.

Ownership: DSL (503) 888-5558
Size: 4,400 acres   **Closest Town:** Charleston

Description: Coastal forest, beaches, dunes, wetlands, and the Coquille River offer habitat for a variety of seabirds, shorebirds, and songbirds. Bandon Marsh, located on the Coquille River estuary across the river from the park, is one of the best areas on the coast for viewing migratory shorebirds.

Viewing Information: Walk along the river, or drive to Coquille Lighthouse at the river's mouth. Watch for sanderlings on the beach. Western gulls, cormorants, and great blue herons may be seen from along the river's edge. Bandon Marsh provides important habitat for Canada geese, green-winged teal, mallard, American wigeon, northern pintail, scoter, bufflehead, and red-breasted merganser. Scan the area from the park with binoculars for ducks and geese during winter.

Directions: *The park is 2 miles north of Bandon on U.S. Highway 101. The refuge is directly across the river from the park.*

Ownership: OPRD, USFWS (503) 347-2209, 867-4550
Size: 1,289 acres; 303 acres   **Closest Town:** Bandon

23 NEW RIVER

Description: The New River flows north for nine miles, separated from the ocean by a single dune, before emptying into the sea. Flowing through upland shrub, sandflats, wetlands, mudflats, estuary, meadow, and pasture, the river and its environs are home to raccoon, black-tailed deer, brush rabbit, coyote, river otter, beaver, and harbor seal. Birds to watch for here include blue-winged and cinnamon teal, bufflehead, brown pelican, greater and lesser yellowlegs, snowy plover, sanderling, bald eagle, peregrine falcon, great horned owl, California quail, violet-green swallow, and American goldfinch. The river also harbors western pond turtle, Pacific tree frog, and chinook salmon.

Viewing Information: Early mornings and evenings from May through October are best for viewing mammals, shorebirds, and waterfowl. The best strategy for finding wildlife here is to walk the trail system from Storm Ranch, visit the viewing sites, and scan the grassy edges or open water for ducks, herons, and other shorebirds. Deer, rabbit, beaver, and otter are often seen here.

Directions: *From Bandon drive south 8.3 miles on U.S. Highway 101. Turn west on Croft Lake Road. Continue 1.5 miles until pavement ends. Continue straight on one-lane dirt road about 0.3 mile to Storm Ranch.*

Ownership: BLM (503) 756-0100
Size: 863 acres   **Closest Town:** Langlois

REGION 2: KLAMATH MOUNTAINS

Encompassing most of southwest Oregon, including the coast, this region of remote, rugged mountains contains the world's most diverse coniferous forest. Douglas-fir, incense-cedar, knobcone pine, Jeffrey pine, lodgepole pine, Port Orford-cedar, foxtail pine, and the coast redwood are just some of the area's native trees. Because of the region's relatively moderate climatic conditions, plants from the northwest, California, inland, and coastal areas all flourish here.

Photo, opposite page: Hemlock forest, Kalmiopsis Widerness Area. **GERRY ELLIS**

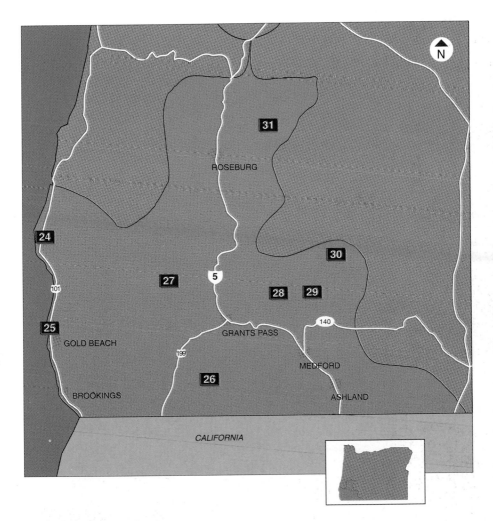

Wildlife Viewing Sites

24	Cape Blanco State Park
25	Rogue River Mouth
26	Oregon Caves National Monument
27	Upper Rogue River
28	Upper and Lower Table Rocks
29	Denman Wildlife Area
30	McGregor Park and Cole Rivers Fish Hatchery
31	Deadline Falls Fish Overlook

24 CAPE BLANCO STATE PARK

Description: An ideal location for whale watching, this park's habitat includes sandy beach, rugged headlands, a Sitka spruce and shore pine forest, beaver marsh, and the Sixes River estuary. Black-tailed deer are common here. Also watch for porcupines and brush rabbits. Birds include red-tailed hawk, California quail, and shorebirds typical of the Oregon coast. Peregrine falcons have been released here in an effort to reintroduce them to the area.

Viewing Information: Watch for migrating gray whales from March through May and from November through December from headlands with good ocean views. It is also possible to see whales during summer from the 12-mile stretch of coast from Cape Blanco south to Humbug Mountain. Calm, overcast days give best visibility. Look for blows, which spout up to 12 feet into the air. If a blow is sighted, look carefully, because more whales are sure to be nearby. Look for harbor seals at the mouth of the Sixes River.

Directions: *Drive north on U.S. Highway 101 from Port Orford to Cape Blanco Road. Turn west on Cape Blanco Road and go 5 miles to park.*

Ownership: OPRD (503) 332-6774
Size: 1,894 acres **Closest Town:** Port Orford

Nearly extirpated by commercial whaling, federal protection has allowed the gray whale to recover, with populations now approaching original levels. Watch for gray whales in November and December as they make their 6,000-mile journey from the Chuckchi and Bering seas to their calving grounds along the Mexican coast. From March through May, they may be seen making the return trip.
JIM YUSKAVITCH

25 ROGUE RIVER MOUTH

Description: River, estuary, sandy beach, and ocean habitats come together here, where the Rogue River meets the sea. Look for harbor seals, California sea lions, and river otters in the water. Waterfowl and shorebirds are common, including great blue heron, egret, brown pelican, scoter, scaup, American wigeon, merganser, and cormorant.

Viewing Information: The best viewing is in the vicinity of the north or south jetty. Upriver viewing is available at Jot's Resort. Harbor seals may be seen year-round between jetties or hauled out on sand spits at low tide. Look for sea lions in these areas during fall, winter, and spring. River otter reside here year-round and are occasionally seen in the river near the resort. Look for herons and egrets foraging along the riverbank. Ospreys patrol the river from spring through fall. Pelicans may be seen along the river and offshore during summer and fall. Scoter, scaup, wigeon, merganser, and cormorant are seen year-round.

Directions: The mouth of the Rogue River is on the north end of Gold Beach, off U.S. Highway 101. Jot's Resort is located 1 mile upriver.

Ownership: ACE, DSL, Port of Gold Beach, Pvt (503) 247-6676 (resort)
Size: 65 acres   **Closest Town:** Gold Beach

26 OREGON CAVES NATIONAL MONUMENT

Description: Three miles of marble caves lie beneath an old-growth forest. Nine species of bats inhabit the caves, including the rare Townsend's big-eared bat. A half-mile of cave is open to the public by guided tour. A fee is charged.

Viewing Information: Take the cave tour to see bats. Although not always visible, bats are present in the cave from October through April. The largest concentrations of bats are found during the winter months.

Directions: From Cave Junction, go 19 miles south on Oregon Highway 46, following signs to monument. The road is winding and paved for the last 8 miles. Travel trailers are not recommended.

Ownership: NPS (503) 592-2100
Size: 480 acres   **Closest Town:** Cave Junction

27 UPPER ROGUE RIVER

Description: Federally designated as a wild and scenic river for much of its length, the Rogue features deep wilderness, wild whitewater, steep canyons, cliffs, grassland, coniferous forest, oak woodlands, marsh, and riparian habitat. From selected viewpoints and trails it is possible to see a wide variety of mammals, birds, and fish.

Viewing Information: Spring and summer are the best times to view wildlife here. Riparian habitat, ponds, and a beaver-dammed creek at Whitehorse Park offer opportunities to see western pond turtles and mallards, Canada geese, and common mergansers. Ospreys and great blue herons nest in the area. Look for the yellow warbler and yellow-breasted chat in willow and alder thickets. Mammals include black-tailed deer and ground squirrel. River otter, fox, raccoon, and beaver are also present but infrequently seen. Easy trails along flat terrain lead throughout the area. From the Hellgate Overlook, scan the canyon cliffs with binoculars for cliff swallows and the river below for ospreys. Hike two miles on the Rogue River Trail in April, May, or August to observe chinook salmon jumping the falls as they journey upstream to spawn.

Directions: *To reach Whitehorse Park, go 3.8 miles south from Merlin on Robertson Bridge Road to Lower River Road. Go south on Lower River Road 4.8 miles to park. Hellgate Overlook is located on the Merlin-Galice Road, 6.5 miles west of Merlin. Rogue River Trail is an additional 6.3 miles west of Hellgate Overlook. Parking and trailhead are at bridge.*

Ownership: BLM (503) 770-2200
Size: NA   **Closest Town:** Merlin

A large, bulky nest of sticks, perched atop a snag overlooking a river or lake, is one of the best indicators that opreys are present. A lucky viewer may watch as this raptor hovers overhead, then suddenly plunges into the water, to emerge with a fish—its primary prey—clutched firmly in its talons.
LEONARD LEE RUE III

Description: Table Rocks rise 800 feet above the valley of the Rogue River. Habitat types range from oak savanna and chaparral to woodland. Vernal pools on the summits and a profusion of wildflowers in the spring add to the area's uniqueness. A diversity of wildlife lives here, including black-tailed deer, coyote, dusky-footed woodrat, California vole, and valley pocket gopher. Birds to watch for include turkey vulture, red-tailed hawk, northern harrier, acorn woodpecker, blue-gray gnatcatcher, western meadowlark, lark and savanna sparrow, and scrub jay. Underfoot watch for western fence lizard, Pacific tree frog, and western rattlesnake. *POISON OAK IS VERY COMMON ALONG THE TRAILS.*

Viewing Information: March through May are the best times to visit. Deer and coyote are found throughout the area. They are most often seen in early morning and evening. Acorn woodpeckers frequent oak savannas. Scrub jays are common in oak and chaparral. Listen and look for rufous-sided towhees in dense brush. Western meadowlarks and sparrows can be found on summits and grassland areas. Western fence lizards are often seen sunning on rocks and logs. From April through May, thousands of Pacific tree frog tadpoles may be seen in the vernal pools.

Directions: *Take Exit 32 off of Interstate 5 at Medford. Go east 1 mile, then turn north on Table Rock Road. To reach Upper Table Rock, turn right on Modoc Road (about 1 mile past Tou Velle State Park), and go 1.5 miles to the fenced trailhead on the west side of the road. To reach Lower Table Rock, turn west on Wheeler Road (about 3 miles past Tou Velle State Park). The fenced trailhead is on the west side of the road.*

Ownership: BLM, The Nature Conservancy, Pvt. (503) 770-2385 (BLM)
Size: 3,022 acres   **Closest Town:** Medford

Pacific tree frogs are found throughout the state and occupy habitats including ponds, lakes, marshes, slackwater streams, and water-filled ditches. Their coloration varies from black and brown to tan, gray, and green. They are capable of changing their hue in a matter of minutes. Look for them in low-growing vegetation near water. GERRY ELLIS

29 DENMAN WILDLIFE AREA

Description: Bordered by the Rogue River and Table Rocks, this area provides habitat for many species of birds, mammals, reptiles, and amphibians. Numerous shallow ponds and riparian areas bordering the Rogue River and Little Butte Creek contain a rich diversity of birds, including great blue heron, western grebe, pied-billed grebe, Canada geese, mallard, pintails, cinnamon teal, lesser scaup, American coot, and common snipe. Raptors to watch for are red-tailed hawk and American kestrel. Forest residents include flicker, rock and mourning dove, acorn woodpecker, hairy and downy woodpecker, raven, and white-breasted nuthatch. Also watch for western gray squirrel, black-tailed jackrabbit, black-tailed deer, bullfrog, and garter and gopher snake.

Viewing Information: Fall and winter are best seasons for viewing waterfowl, hawks, and eagles. Drive Tou Velle Road along the Rogue River, Military Slough, and ponds for great blue herons, ducks, geese, and other waterfowl. The concentration of ponds and sloughs near area headquarters is also a good bet for waterfowl. Ospreys and kingfishers cruise the river for fish. Numerous songbirds can be seen in wet bottomland habitats, especially in spring. Look for western gray squirrel and acorn woodpecker in oak forest areas. Black-tailed deer may be seen throughout the area mornings and evenings. Frogs and garter snakes are found in wet areas, along ponds and sloughs.

Directions: *From Medford, drive north 6 miles on Oregon Highway 62. Turn west onto Agate Road, which is the eastern boundary of the wildlife area. Turn west onto East Gregory Road and follow to area headquarters.*

Ownership: ODFW (503) 826-8774
Size: 1,799 acres   **Closest Town:** White City

A subspecies of the mule deer that roams the eastern half of Oregon, the black-tailed deer is most often seen in open areas and forest edges during early morning and evening hours, westward from the crest of the Cascade Mountains.

ERWIN & PEGGY BAUER

30 MCGREGOR PARK AND COLE RIVERS FISH HATCHERY

Description: Steep rocky slopes, river bottom, riparian habitat, and mixed oak and conifer forest characterize this park and hatchery located 153 miles upstream from the mouth of the Rogue River. Bird life is varied, including osprey, belted kingfisher, great blue heron, merganser, scaup, mallard, ring-necked duck, bufflehead, and common goldeneye. The hatchery contains chinook and coho salmon, steelhead, kokanee, and rainbow trout.

Viewing Information: Belted kingfisher and great blue heron are seen year-round, osprey from March through October. November through March is best for observing waterfowl. Occasional bald or golden eagle. Visitors may watch hatchery staff hand-spawn fish from late September to May.

Directions: *From Medford, drive north about 30 miles on Oregon Highway 62. Turn left on Takelma Drive and follow signs to Cole Rivers Fish Hatchery, Lost Creek Dam, and McGregor Park Visitor Center.*

Ownership: ACE, ODFW (503) 878-2255, 878-2235
Size: 89 acres   **Closest Town:** Shady Cove

31 DEADLINE FALLS FISH OVERLOOK

Description: A prime place to see Chinook salmon and steelhead trout leaping the falls as they journey upriver to their spawning grounds. The Deadline Falls Trail winds through a forest of old-growth Douglas-fir, red cedar, and sugar pine to a viewing platform overlooking the falls.

Viewing Information: Walk the easy, 400-yard trail from the parking lot to the viewing platform. June through October is the peak period for fish migration. The fish are most apt to be active in the mornings and late afternoons. However, with patience, fish may be seen at any time of day. Watch for osprey along the river from March through August.

Directions: *Located 20 miles east of Roseburg off of Oregon Highway 138. From Idleyld Park, go 1.3 miles east to the Swiftwater Bridge. Turn south and cross the bridge. Parking lot is on the left. Trail begins at North Umpqua Trailhead on north side of lot. Sign along trail directs hikers to viewing area.*

Ownership: BLM (503) 440-4930
Size: 1 acre   **Closest Town:** Idleyld Park

REGION 3: WILLAMETTE VALLEY

This broad interior valley, now extensively developed and converted to agriculture, reveals only remnants of the oak savannas, grasslands, beaver marsh, and cottonwood, alder, and willow-lined streams that existed here before white settlement. Yet much remains. Beavers still ply marshland waters at dusk and the dawn air is filled with the honks of thousands of Canada geese, down from Alaska for the winter, as they descend to the refuge of a grainfield.

Photo, opposite page: Cabell Marsh, William L. Finley National Wildlife Refuge.
JIM YUSKAVITCH

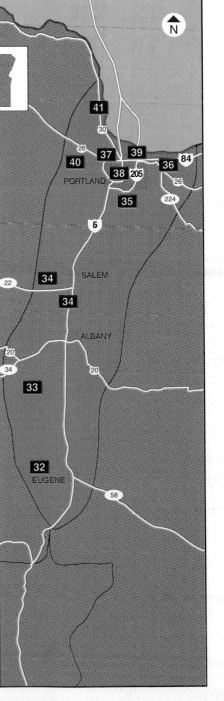

Wildlife Viewing Sites

32 Fern Ridge Wildlife Area
33 William L. Finley National
    Wildlife Refuge
34 Ankeny and Baskett Slough
    National Wildlife Refuges
35 Molalla River State Park
36 Oxbow Park
37 Metro Washington Park Zoo
38 Audubon Society of Portland
39 Tryon Creek State Park
40 Jackson Bottom Wetlands Preserve
41 Sauvie Island Wildlife Area

32 FERN RIDGE WILDLIFE AREA

Description: This site contains extensive marshes, grasslands, shrublands, and forests surrounding Fern Ridge Reservoir. More than 250 species of birds have been documented here. Bird species to look for include nesting osprey, short-eared owl, black-shouldered kite, yellow-headed blackbird, and marsh wren. Black-tailed deer, beaver, mink, fox, and coyote live here. Also watch for western pond turtle, ring-necked snake, and rubber boa.

Viewing Information: Large concentrations of migratory waterfowl, including ducks, geese, swans, egrets, and various shorebirds, can be seen here in fall and winter. Viewing opportunities for migratory waterfowl, wading birds, and shorebirds are especially good during winter months. Spring and summer are best for nesting osprey and songbirds. Scan the tall grass in marshy areas for yellow-headed blackbirds. Short-eared owls are most likely to be seen in the evenings as they make low-level sorties over open grasslands. Look for acorn woodpeckers in the oak forests. Flocks of barn and violet-green swallows and purple martins swoop over open water as they feed on insects in the evenings. Black-tailed deer, great blue heron, and bald eagle are present year-round.

Directions: From Eugene, drive 6 miles west on Oregon Highway 126 (West 11th). Clear Lake Road borders the area on the north.

Ownership: ACE (503) 935-2591 (ODFW)
Size: 17,726 acres   **Closest Town:** Eugene

Over 250 species of birds have been documented at Fern Ridge Wildlife Area. This site encompasses over 12,000 acres of open water, marsh, grasslands, and woodlands. Large concentrations of waterfowl gather here during peak nesting and migration seasons. WAYNE MORROW/FERN RIDGE WILDLIFE AREA

Description: Established to protect the dusky Canada goose, this refuge's mix of marsh, oak and ash woodlands, croplands, hedgerows, and Douglas-fir forest also harbors many other species of wildlife. Black-tailed deer, coyote, beaver, and even the occasional black bear roam here. Uplands harbor ruffed grouse, California and mountain quail, and numerous songbirds. Wood duck and common merganser nest here. Large numbers of waterfowl, particularly Canada geese, congregate during winter months. Flocks of ducks attract raptors, notably bald eagles and rare peregrine falcon. Most of the refuge is closed to foot traffic from November 1 to April 15, but wildlife may be viewed from refuge roads. Woodpecker Loop interpretive trail is open year-round.

Viewing Information: Winter is the best time to see geese, when they concentrate in large flocks in open fields. Also watch for raptors in winter. Spring, summer, and fall are best for other waterfowl, shorebirds, wading birds, and songbirds. McFadden's Marsh is an excellent spot for ducks, great blue herons, egrets, long-billed marsh wrens, red-winged blackbirds, barn swallows, and a variety of warblers. Northern harriers can be seen making low-level flights over fields and grasslands. Look for short-eared owls and deer in the same areas at dusk. Beaver are sometimes seen at Cabell Marsh in the evenings.

Directions: From Corvallis, drive 11 miles south on Oregon Highway 99W. Turn right and follow signs to refuge.

Ownership: USFWS (503) 757-7236
Size: 5,325 acres   **Closest Town:** Corvallis

The V-shaped formations of Canada geese in flight are a common sight throughout Oregon, where thousands of these "honkers" are full-time residents, and even more pass through on their annual migrations. Although most populations of Canada geese are healthy and growing, the Aleutian Canada goose, a subspecies that winters in Oregon, is federally-listed as threatened.

LEONARD LEE RUE III

34 ANKENY AND BASKETT SLOUGH NATIONAL WILDLIFE REFUGES

Description: Part of the Willamette Valley National Wildlife Refuge System, these areas of cropland, marshes, and woodland provide critical winter habitat for the dusky Canada goose. Many other species of waterfowl also winter on these refuges. Baskett Slough is closed to foot travel from October 1 to May 1 and Ankeny is closed from November 1 to April 15. Wildlife may be viewed from the refuge roads year-round.

Viewing Information: Winter is best for seeing the large flocks of Canada geese that winter here. Look for them in open fields. Viewpoints are available in both refuges.

Directions: *To reach Ankeny, take the Talbot exit off of Interstate 5. Travel north on Jorgenson Road to Wintel Road. Drive west on Wintel Road to refuge. To reach Baskett Slough, drive west 12 miles on Oregon Highway 99W from Salem. Continue west 1.5 miles on Oregon Highway 22 to refuge.*

Ownership: USFWS (503) 757-7236
Size: 2,796; 2,492 acres   **Closest Town:** Albany, Rickreall

35 MOLALLA RIVER STATE PARK

Description: Groves of cottonwoods mark the confluence of the Molalla, Pudding, and Willamette rivers. The trees are home to one of the largest great blue heron rookeries in the Willamette Valley. Riverside habitat also harbors nesting ospreys, as well as mallard, cinnamon teal, and other ducks.

Viewing Information: Herons nest here from February through July. The rookery is on an island in the Molalla River. Look for platforms of sticks in the cottonwood trees. They can be viewed from the parking lot, or by boat from the river. Stay a respectful distance from the rookery to avoid disturbing the herons. Osprey glide above the rivers during spring and summer. Ducks are most common during winter.

Directions: *From Canby, drive northwest on Holly St. about 2 miles.*

Ownership: OPRD (503) 678-1251
Size: 567 acres   **Closest Town:** Canby

36 OXBOW PARK

Description: Old-growth and second growth Douglas-fir forest, floodplain, and the Sandy River combine to make this area an excellent place to experience nature. The river attracts osprey, great blue heron, American dipper, and common merganser. Pileated woodpeckers drill for insects in the old-growth forest, where black-tailed deer and beaver roam.

Viewing Information: Black-tailed deer are sometimes seen in early mornings and evenings in open areas and along the Sandy River. Watch for dippers on rocks and logs in fast-moving water and for mergansers as they make low-level flights up and downstream. Kingfishers perch on alders along the river's banks. Shallow spots in the river are good places to look for great blue herons. Scanning flatwater areas of the river at dusk may turn up a beaver. Chickarees (Douglas' squirrel) are most often seen in campgrounds. Old-growth forest areas are likely spots for pileated woodpeckers. Chinook salmon spawn by the hundreds in the river during September and October.

Directions: From Portland, drive east on Interstate 84. Take Exit 17 (Troutdale). Continue past truckstop to 257th Avenue. Turn right and go 4 miles to Division Street. Turn left and follow signs 6 miles to park.

Ownership: Multnomah County (503) 663-4708
Size: 1,000 acres   **Closest Town:** Gresham

37 METRO WASHINGTON PARK ZOO

Description: Animals from throughout the world may be viewed in simulated natural surroundings. Exhibits include elephants, big cats, bears, penguins, primates, African rainforest, Alaskan tundra, and wildlife habitat and butterfly gardens. Of special interest is the Cascade Exhibit, which was rated as the best new exhibit in the U.S. in 1983.

Viewing Information: Visit the Cascade Exhibit, which includes a 400-yard trail through a deep ravine and native vegetation. Special windows allow underwater viewing of aquatic species of Oregon wildlife. Other highlights are a beaver dam, aquarium and terrarium exhibits, and a walk-through marsh aviary. Also visit the adjacent elk meadow to view Roosevelt elk.

Directions: The zoo is located at 4001 SW Canyon Road, just west of Portland off of U.S. Highway 26.

Ownership: Portland Metro (503) 226-1561
Size: 62 acres   **Closest Town:** Portland

OREGON BIODIVERSITY:
OF BEAVERS AND PIONEERS

The richest wildlife habitats are often the most attractive places for human settlement. With its gentle climate and fertile soil, the Willamette Valley was the "Promised Land" to pioneers who crossed the United States in covered wagons during the 1840s. When settlers first arrived, they found a landscape of oak woodland, grassland, and numerous marshes and streams choked with vegetation. Beavers were abundant, and their dam building created new wetlands, providing waterfowl with nesting habitat and sanctuary.

While many wildlife species still thrive here, most of the Willamette Valley's original habitat has been urbanized, or converted to such single-crop agriculture as grass seed farms.

38 AUDUBON SOCIETY OF PORTLAND

Description: This woodland sanctuary is home to a variety of songbirds, mammals, reptiles, and amphibians. Features include a pond, creek, four miles of trails, a nature center, wildlife rehabilitation center, and bookstore. Classes and field trips are available. The bird list includes the wood duck, band-tailed pigeon, mourning dove, pileated woodpecker, Steller's jay, black-capped chickadee, chestnut-backed chickadee, red-breasted nuthatch, winter wrens, varied thrush, rufous-sided towhee, orange-crowned warbler, black-headed grosbeak, evening grosbeak, and song sparrow. Also watch for northwestern garter snake, western pond turtle, and rough-skinned newt. Black-tailed deer are occasionally seen.

Viewing Information: April and May are the peak months for migrating songbirds. Reptiles can be found during the summer months; look for rough-skinned newts breeding in the pond. The creek holds native cutthroat trout. In winter, nature center bird feeders are prime spots to view nuthatches, towhees, woodpeckers, jays, chickadees, and varied thrushes. Resident barn owls, pygmy owls, acorn woodpeckers, and red-tailed hawks may be seen at the rehabilitation center along with wildlife rehabilitation activities.

Directions: From Portland, drive west on N.W. Lovejoy past N.W. 25th. Road bears to right and becomes N.W. Cornell Road. Continue 1.5 miles through two tunnels. Sanctuary is on right 0.5 mile past second tunnel.

Ownership: Audubon Society of Portland (503) 292-6855
Size: 160 acres   **Closest Town:** Portland

The dark-eyed junco is a commonly-seen resident of deciduous and coniferous forests, fields, and roadside shrubs, as well as suburban yards and parks. Flocks of these small birds are often observed during the winter months as they flit from tree to tree in a western Oregon forest.
ERWIN & PEGGY BAUER

Description: A second-growth Douglas-fir forest interspersed with western hemlock, grand fir, and western red cedar dominates this state park. A lush forest understory of wildflowers, ferns, and salal along with stands of red alder, black cottonwood, and Oregon ash along Tryon Creek completes the picture. Birds of the forest include pileated woodpecker, red-breasted nuthatch, robin, and Steller's jay. Also watch for Townsend's chipmunk and Douglas' squirrel. A nature center and hiking, bicycling, and equestrian trails are present.

Viewing Information: Although birds can be seen year-round, activity peaks in spring. Walk the forest trails. Look for woodpeckers and nuthatches around dead snags. Steller's jays are seen throughout the forest. Listen and watch for Douglas' squirrels chattering in the trees. Beaver live in Tryon Creek, but visitors are more likely to see great blue herons wading in shallow pools. An occasional black-tailed deer is seen here. Scan the creek bottom carefully for the reddish shapes of crayfish. Trilliums and other forest wildflowers are in full bloom from March through May. Watch for rough-skinned newts on the trails during and after rains from fall through spring.

Directions: From Portland, take Exit 297 off of Interstate 5 to Terwilliger Blvd. Follow Terwilliger Blvd. through the intersections with Taylors Ferry and Boones Ferry roads. Follow signs past Northwestern School of Law. Park entrance is 1 mile south on right.

Ownership: OPRD (503) 653-3166
Size: 635 acres **Closest Town:** Portland

The school guide program is a popular activity for teachers and students alike, as volunteers lead them on educational nature tours through Tryon Creek State Park.

TRYON CREEK STATE PARK

40 JACKSON BOTTOM WETLANDS PRESERVE

Description: Bordered by the Tualatin River on the south, this site contains wetlands, freshwater marsh, sloughs, ponds, and forested wetlands. Winter flooding is supplemented during summer by treated wastewater from the nearby Hillsboro Wastewater Treatment Plant, ensuring year-round wetland habitat for wildlife. Two sites offer good viewing along the preserve's western boundary: one on the north end, by the wastewater treatment plant, and another at the southern boundary. There is no road access into the preserve. Birdwatchers will enjoy hiking the mile-long Kingfisher Marsh Interpretive Trail, which leads from the south viewsite along the Tualatin River to Kingfisher Marsh.

Viewing Information: The preserve provides habitat to 130 species of birds including waterfowl, songbirds, hawks, and shorebirds. Winter is an especially good time to observe migrating birds. Such water-loving mammals as otter, mink, beaver, and raccoon may be seen along the interpretive trail. The preserve also harbors a great blue heron rookery.

Directions: *Travel south from Hillsboro on Oregon Highway 219 about 7 blocks past Baseline Street. The site is on the left, next to the Hillsboro Wastewater Treatment Plant.*

Ownership: City of Hillsboro, Unified Sewerage Agency (503) 681-6206
Size: 650 acres   **Closest Town:** Hillsboro

Wetlands, including those at Jackson Bottom Wetlands Preserve, provide critical habitat for many species of fish and other wildlife, and improve water quality in nearby rivers by filtering out nutrients, chemical and organic wastes, and reducing sediment levels. The lower 48 states have now lost over half of their historic wetland areas to human enroachment. JACKSON BOTTOM

Description: This area contains rolling uplands and numerous shallow lakes interspersed with cottonwood, willow, ash, and canary grass swales, all within the Columbia River floodplain. An important stop for migrating waterfowl, the area's wetlands provide ideal habitat. During fall migration, up to 150,000 ducks and geese gather on the island. Wood ducks, dusky Canada geese, sandhill cranes, bald eagles, and great blue herons are just some of the birds seen here. Mammals include black-tailed deer, mink, red fox, raccoon, and beaver. Viewing platforms and interpretive areas are available. A parking fee is charged. To protect wildlife, entry into the area is restricted from October through April. Check at headquarters for details.

Viewing Information: Wood ducks are most likely seen March through May. The best time for American wigeon, northern shoveler, bufflehead, ruddy duck, green-winged teal, and common merganser is September through March. Sandhill cranes are present September to November and February through March. Great blue herons are seen year-round. Look for bald eagles from December through March. Best time to see Canada geese is October through April. Look for ducks and herons in wetland areas and for geese and cranes in wetlands and fields. Search for yellow warblers, common yellowthroats, Wilson's warblers, and orange-crowned warblers in wet swales and thickets during spring. Deer are most likely to be seen morning and evenings. Watch open water and marshy areas in the evening for beaver.

Directions: To reach headquarters, drive west 10 miles from downtown Portland on U.S. Highway 30. Cross Sauvie Island Bridge and travel north for 2 miles. Headquarters is on the right just past NW Reeder Road junction.

Ownership: ODFW (503) 621-3488
Size: 12,000 acres   **Closest Town:** Portland

Considered by many to be the most beautiful of all ducks, wood ducks live in wooded areas near rivers, swamps, and ponds. They nest in tree cavities and have sharp claws, enabling them to perch on branches and stumps. Small flocks of these handsome birds are often seen near dusk during autumn, as they return from feeding areas to their nighttime roosts.
ALAN & SANDY CAREY

REGION 4: CASCADE MOUNTAINS

Born of fire, the extinct or merely dormant volcanic peaks of Oregon's major mountain range tower over ten thousand feet above sea level. Even the lesser mountains reach to eight and nine thousand feet. Below icy peaks, snowfields, and perpetually frozen glaciers lie alpine meadows, and below them, deep coniferous forest. Moist, westside fir and hemlock forest gives way to ponderosa pine and the dry east slope. Black-tailed deer roam the west slope, mule deer the east, and mountain lions steal through the dark pines and firs, stalking them both.

Photo, opposite page: Sparks Lake, Mount Bachelor, Deschutes National Forest. **FRED PFLUGHOFT**

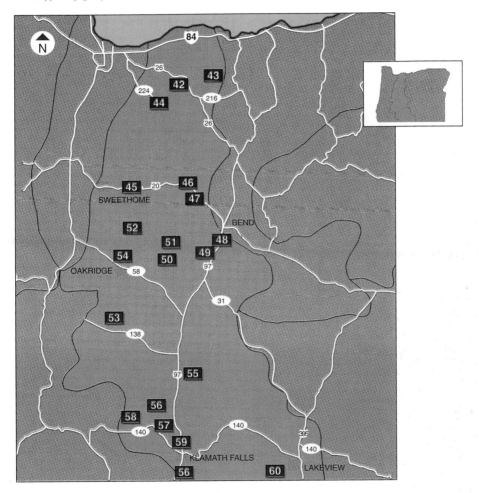

Wildlife Viewing Sites

42	Little Crater Lake and Little Crater Meadow
43	White River Wildlife Area
44	Chinook Salmon Spawning Overlook
45	Walton Ranch Interpretive Trail
46	Metolius Fish Overlook
47	Cold Springs
48	The High Desert Museum
49	Sunriver Nature Center
50	Davis Lake
51	Crane Prairie Reservoir
52	McKenzie River
53	Marster's Bridge and Soda Springs Fish Overlooks
54	Buckhead Wildlife Area
55	Klamath Marsh National Wildlife Refuge
56	Upper and Lower Klamath National Wildlife Refuges
57	Eagle Ridge Park
58	Whiskey Springs Interpretive Trail
59	Link River Nature Trail
60	Dog Lake

42 LITTLE CRATER LAKE AND LITTLE CRATER MEADOW

Description: This tiny artesian spring-fed lake is surrounded by a large wet mountain meadow. A paved 300-yard trail leads from Little Crater Lake Campground to Little Crater lake.

Viewing Information: June and July are the best months to visit. Walk the trail from the campground to the lake in the morning and search the brush around the lake for warblers. Continue along the trail beyond the lake and through the fence gate and scan willows and alders along the creek and wet meadows for yellowthroats, yellow warblers, hermit warblers, and red-winged blackbirds. Continue on the trail to the edge of the forest for Steller's and gray jays. During evenings, large numbers of nighthawks swoop over the open meadows. Also watch for deer and elk near dusk.

Directions: From the junction of U.S. Highway 26 and Oregon Highway 35, drive east on U.S. 26 for 8.2 miles. Turn south on Skyline Road (Forest Service Road 42). Go 3.6 miles. Turn right on Abbot Road (Forest Service Road 58). Continue 2.3 miles and turn right into Little Crater Lake Campground. The trail begins on the west edge of the campground loop road.

Ownership: USFS (503) 328-6211
Size: 150 acres   **Closest Town:** Government Camp

43 WHITE RIVER WILDLIFE AREA

Description: Sagebrush flats and forests of oak and mature ponderosa pine characterize this area where herds of black-tailed deer and Rocky Mountain elk roam. A network of primitive roads winds throughout the area. High-clearance vehicles may be needed on some roads. Other roads within the area are closed for the protection of wildlife. *RATTLESNAKES ARE FOUND HERE.*

Viewing Information: Black-tailed deer, elk, wild turkey, Lewis' woodpecker, and western gray squirrel are the wildlife most likely to be seen here. Slowly drive area roads. Spring through fall are best seasons for squirrels, woodpeckers, and turkeys. Look for them in oak forests. In winter, watch for elk and deer along forest edges and open areas at dawn and dusk.

Directions: From Tygh Valley, follow signs for Wamic, traveling 5.4 miles on Wamic Market Road. At Wamic, bear right onto Dodson Road. Go about 2 miles, following signs for wildlife area office. Turn left just before Camp Morrow sign. Follow gravel road 2.2 miles to headquarters on left.

Ownership: ODFW (503) 544-2126
Size: 41,301 acres   **Closest Town:** Wamic

44 CHINOOK SALMON SPAWNING OVERLOOK

Description: The upper Clackamas, a national wild and scenic river, offers an excellent opportunity to view spawning chinook salmon each fall. A trail overlooking the river leads from the Riverside Campground through a lush forest of Douglas-fir, western red cedar, western hemlock, and vine maple. During the peak of the spawning season, Forest Service staff are available to answer questions at the Ripplebrook Ranger Station and at the overlook.

Viewing Information: Chinook salmon spawn in the large pool about 2,000 feet downstream from Riverside Campground from mid-September through the first week of October. Follow the trail a short distance to a high point and view from the cliff overlooking the river. *STAY BACK FROM THE EDGE.*

Directions: *From Estacada, drive 29 miles southeast on Oregon Highway 224, which eventually becomes Forest Road 46. Turn right into Riverside Campground. The Riverside Trailhead is on the north end of the campground. There is also a pullout on Forest Road 46, 2.5 miles southeast of Ripplebrook Ranger Station where spawning salmon may be viewed.*

Ownership: USFS (503) 630-4256
Size: 0.25 acres **Closest Town:** Estacada

45 WALTON RANCH INTERPRETIVE TRAIL

Description: A resident herd of Roosevelt elk graze on this pastureland during winter months. The pasture, on the south side of the South Santiam River, is surrounded by steep ridges blanketed with Douglas-fir and red alder.

Viewing Information: Elk can be seen here from December through May. Early mornings and evenings are best. The best viewpoint is from the platforms on the interpretive trail. Park at the Trout Creek trailhead and follow the signs to the viewing platforms. The 400-yard walk is barrier free and includes interpretive signs.

Directions: *Drive 20 miles east of Sweet Home on U.S. Highway 20. Look for signs for Trout Creek Trailhead on north side of highway.*

Ownership: USFS (503) 367-5168
Size: 25 acres **Closest Town:** Sweet Home

46 METOLIUS FISH OVERLOOK

Description: The Metolius River rises fully formed from underground springs and flows through a forest of ponderosa pine, fir, and cedar. Large rainbow trout are regularly seen in its clear waters from the observation platform at Camp Sherman. An interpretive kiosk provides information on the area and its fish residents.

Viewing Information: Rainbow trout are visible year-round from the observation deck. Look in the deep pool immediately below the platform, just upstream from the bridge. The fish will usually be facing upstream, ready to catch any food that may float by. Kokanee salmon migrate upstream from Lake Billy Chinook to spawn in September and October. Their bright red spawning colors make them easy to spot. Osprey are common along the river, especially at nearby Wizard Falls Fish Hatchery.

Directions: *From Sisters, travel west 9 miles on U.S. Highway 20. Turn right at sign for Camp Sherman/Metolius River. Bear left at fork at milepost 2.6. At stop sign, turn right onto Forest Service Road 1419 to Camp Sherman. Viewing site and parking are on right immediately across bridge. To reach hatchery, bear right at milepost 2.6 fork. Hatchery is about 6.5 miles on left.*

Ownership: USFS (503) 549-2111
Size: 0.25 acre   **Closest Town:** Sisters

47 COLD SPRINGS

Description: This large grove of quaking aspens surrounded by old-growth ponderosa pine offers excellent opportunities to see many species of birds common to the dry, eastern slope of the Cascade Mountains. Birds that winter in Central and South America, as well as year-round residents, may be seen during the course of a morning's walk. Birds likely to be seen include MacGillivray's, yellow-rumped, and yellow warbler; black-capped and mountain chickadee; pygmy and red-breasted nuthatch; and hairy, white-headed, downy, and pileated woodpecker. Keep an eye out for the seldom-seen black-backed woodpecker. A trail parallels a spring-fed stream beside the aspen grove. Cold Springs campground is adjacent to the site.

Viewing Information: Birds are most active May through August. Look for all of the above birds in aspen grove. Early morning and evening are best.

Directions: *From Sisters, drive 4 miles west on Oregon Highway 242. Turn right at sign for Cold Springs Campground.*

Ownership: USFS (503) 549-2111
Size: 4 acres   **Closest Town:** Sisters

Description: This is an outstanding museum with indoor and outdoor exhibits on the natural history and cultural heritage of the Intermountain West. Excellent close-up viewing of many captive, native animals in natural surroundings, including river otters, porcupines, Nuttall's cottontail, Ord's kangaroo rat, pallid bats, burrowing, and barn owls, Lahontan cutthroat trout, gopher snakes, rubber boas, and western fence, collared, and leopard lizards. Daily presentations are given on native eagles, hawks, and owls. Classes are offered to the general public. A book and nature store is on-site.

Viewing Information: In addition to the captive animals, many species of free-roaming wildlife may be seen on the museum grounds. Walk the 0.3-mile paved trail through ponderosa pines, along the stream and wetlands. Spring and summer are best for small mammals and birds. Fall brings flocks of migrating songbirds. Gray and Douglas' squirrel, Belding's and golden-mantled ground squirrel, and chipmunk are found throughout the grounds. An occasional mink is seen in wetland areas. Look in the stream for rainbow trout. Pygmy and white-breasted nuthatch, mountain chickadee, and dark-eyed junco may be seen in the pine forest. Evening grosbeak, red crossbill, and California quail are also frequent visitors. The museum's bird feeder station is a productive viewing site during winter months.

Directions: *Drive 4 miles south of Bend on U.S. Highway 97. Look for large museum sign at entrance on east side of road.*

Ownership: Pvt. (503) 382-4754
Size: 150 acres   **Closest Town:** Bend

Come face-to-face with some of the inhabitants of the West's sagebrush country at the High Desert Museum in Bend. This living museum explores the full spectrum of the high desert through exhibits, live animal and pioneer demonstrations, galleries, nature trails, and walk-through slices of history. THE HIGH DESERT MUSEUM

49 SUNRIVER NATURE CENTER

Description: Set amidst a forest of lodgepole and ponderosa pine, this nature center features a lake, marsh, amphitheater, observatory, interpretive programs, live native animals, natural history and historical exhibits, and the only botanical garden in Oregon east of the Cascade Mountains. Birds seen here include Canada geese, mallard, red-winged blackbird, osprey, evening grosbeaks, Cassin's finch, mountain chickadee, Steller's jay, and various sparrows.

Viewing Information: In addition to visiting the nature center, walk the Osgood Nature Trail. Watch for geese, ducks, blackbirds, and osprey in wetland areas. Grosbeaks, finches, chickadees, jays, and sparrows are seen in forested areas. Botanical garden also attracts a variety of songbirds and insects.

Directions: *From Bend, drive south 13 miles on U.S. Highway 97. Turn west at the Sunriver exit. Go right into Sunriver at Center Drive. Take first right onto Abbot Drive. Take second right at Abbot Circle 2, then third right at Abbot Circle 3 to River Road. Nature Center is on right.*

Ownership: Pvt. (503) 593-4394
Size: 7 acres   **Closest Town:** Sunriver

50 DAVIS LAKE

Description: Nestled in the deep forests of the Cascade Mountains, Davis Lake fluctuates wildly in size, depending on the time of year and current rainfall. Geologically young, it was formed when a lava flow blocked off the north end of Odell Creek. Wet meadows ring the lake, important habitat for elk, coyote, and a variety of waterfowl and wading birds.

Viewing Information: Best viewing opportunities are found where Odell Creek enters the lake. Watch for elk and coyote at dawn and dusk, particularly in spring and early summer. Look for osprey perched in trees and soaring over the lake. Meadows and shorelines harbor great blue heron, western grebe, Brewer's blackbird, and many species of ducks. Bald eagles and sandhill cranes nest here. Both are easily disturbed while nesting, so keep a respectful distance. Look for Douglas' squirrel and golden-mantled ground squirrel in the campgrounds. Late winter and spring are best for waterfowl and cranes. Ospreys and eagles are present year-round.

Directions: *From Crescent on U.S. Highway 97, follow signs for Davis Lake west 19 miles. Travel north 8 miles on Forest Service Road 46 to lake. Watch for binocular logo signs at entrance to lake campgrounds. To reach the mouth of Odell Creek, follow signs to East Davis Lake Campground.*

Ownership: USFS (503) 433-2234
Size: 300 to 3,500 acres
Closest Town: Crescent

51 CRANE PRAIRIE RESERVOIR

Description: A large population of bald eagles and ospreys nest on this expansive reservoir high in the Cascade Mountains. Lake, wetlands, meadows, and a surrounding forest of pine, fir, and spruce combine to provide habitat for elk and mule deer. Birds include cormorant, spotted sandpiper, Canada geese, mallard, goldeneye, wood duck, scaup, green-winged teal, American wigeon, and pintail. Cascade spotted frogs live here and the reservoir is renowned for its large rainbow trout.

Viewing Information: Summer is the best viewing season. A number of campgrounds provide access around the lake. A special area is set aside for viewing osprey. Look for eagles and osprey flying over the lake or perched on the many dead snags rising from the water. Ducks and geese raft on the lake's surface. Scan shorelines for sandpipers and other shorebirds. Alert hikers may find a rare Cascade spotted frog in shallow water along the shore. Deer and elk venture into nearby meadows in early evening.

Directions: *From Bend, drive south 15 miles on U.S. Highway 97. Turn right at the Sunriver turnoff (Forest Road 40). Drive 21 miles to Forest Road 46. Go south on Forest Road 46 and watch for campgrounds around reservoir. The osprey viewing trail begins 0.5 mile south of Quinn River Campground on Forest Road 46.*

Ownership: USFS (503) 388-5664
Size: 10,600 acres   **Closest Town:** LaPine

Our national symbol since 1782, the bald eagle has seen some hard times. Primarily a fish eater, it is a bird of rivers, lakes, and sea coast. Illegal shootings, pesticides, and habitat destruction have taken a toll on bald eagle populations. The banning of the pesticide DDT was a critical step in the bird's recovery. Bald eagles are listed as a threatened species in Oregon.

GERRY ELLIS

OREGON BIODIVERSITY:
THE LIFE OF AN ANCIENT FOREST

Ecosystems untouched by human activity contain a remarkable diversity of plant and animal species. Scientists and wildlife experts refer to this wide array of life as "bio-diversity." Nowhere is this concept more evident than in the old-growth forests of the Pacific Northwest.

In these forests, Douglas-firs may be 300 feet tall and 1,000 years old. Young trees grow amidst the towering giants. The forest floor is covered with a variety of herbs and shrubs.

Even after a tree has died, it will continue to sustain life. Standing dead trees provide shelter, nesting space, and food for mammals, birds, and insects. Decaying logs on the forest floor become nurseries for new plant growth, returning nutrients to the soil as they decompose. Logs lying in streams provide habitat for fish and other aquatic creatures.

Many animals, including the northern spotted owl, northern goshawk, pine marten, and northern flying squirrel depend on the unique habitat of old-growth forests. Scientists estimate that only about ten percent of the Pacific Northwest's ancient forests remain.

52 MCKENZIE RIVER

Description: The McKenzie River rushes out of the Cascade Mountains in a series of wild rapids and crystalline pools. Travelers along this forested river stretch may see black-tailed deer, osprey, bald eagles, red-tailed hawks, turkey vultures, common mergansers, mallards, Canada geese, American dippers, and perhaps a rare harlequin duck. Steelhead trout migrate upstream to spawn during the summer months.

Viewing Information: Wildlife may be seen throughout the year along this route. Spring, summer, and fall offer the best viewing of waterfowl. Eagles are best seen in winter—stop at the numerous boat ramps and scan the river and forest edges.

Directions: *Travel east on Oregon Highway 126 from Springfield. The viewing area is located along the river, between the towns of Vida and Blue River.*

Ownership: BLM (503) 947-3334
Size: NA   **Closest Town:** Vida

Mallards belong to the group of ducks called puddle or dabbling ducks for their habit of "tipping up" in shallow water as they feed on aquatic vegetation. They are one of our most common and widely distributed ducks. Mallards may be found in wetlands throughtout Oregon, where the drakes are easily recognized by their bright green head. FRED PFLUGHOFT

Description: Designated as a wild and scenic river, the North Umpqua flows through dense coniferous forests on the western slope of the Cascade Mountains. This is an important river for salmon, trout, and steelhead. Ease of access and crystal clear waters make Marster's Bridge and Soda Springs ideal places to view salmon and steelhead trout migrating upstream to spawning grounds.

Viewing Information: Chinook salmon can be seen spawning at Marster's Bridge during September and October. Look in the pool downstream of the bridge and against the north bank. An occasional black-tailed deer, common merganser, or osprey also may be seen. Beware of steep banks and deep, fast-moving water. At Soda Springs, September and October is best for Chinook salmon. Steelhead trout can be seen during April, May, July, and August. Also watch for resident rainbow and brown trout. Look for fish in the long, deep pool just downstream from the bridge or in riffles above and below the pool.

Directions: Marster's Bridge is about 50 miles east of Roseburg. To reach the bridge, go east on Oregon Highway 138 for 28 miles from Idleyld Park. There are parking turnouts on both sides of the bridge. Use caution as traffic can be heavy at times. To reach Soda Springs, continue east for another 5 miles and turn north at the sign for Soda Springs Reservoir. Bear left onto Soda Springs Road for 1 mile. Cross the bridge and park along the gravel road.

Ownership: USFS (503) 672-6601
Size: 2 acres; 10 acres   **Closest Town:** Idleyld Park

Steelhead are rainbow trout that, like salmon, migrate from the streams of their birth to the ocean, where they mature. They can be seen at Deadline Falls and Soda Springs during the summer months as they return to their natal streams to spawn.

KELLY JAMES

54 BUCKHEAD WILDLIFE AREA

Description: Located along the Middle Fork of the Willamette River, this site presents a typical streamside ecosystem. Willows line the Willamette, giving way to coniferous forests, and blackberry thickets. The lush vegetation provides habitat for mallard, wood duck, osprey, and a variety of songbirds.

Viewing Information: Early summer is the best season to visit. Watch for western pond turtles sunning along the creek. Ducks frequent the creek and river and osprey may be seen overhead. Streamside willows and shrubs are often busy with a variety of warblers. Look for dark-eyed junco, winter wren, Steller's jay, varied thrush, and yellow-bellied sapsucker in wooded areas.

Directions: From Interstate 5 just south of Eugene, drive east 32 miles on Oregon Highway 58. Turn left following signs to Westfir. Turn left again after crossing the Middle Fork Willamette River. Go 1 mile and turn left, following signs to tree nursery. Go 2 miles, past nursery, to wildlife area parking lot on left.

Ownership: USFS (503) 937-2129
Size: 250 acres   **Closest Town:** Oakridge

55 KLAMATH MARSH NATIONAL WILDLIFE REFUGE

Description: This extensive bulrush and wocus marsh provides important nesting and migration resting areas for many species of waterfowl. Surrounding meadows and forests harbor a variety of birds, mammals, and other wildlife. Look for cinnamon teal, mallards, Canada geese, American white pelicans, northern shovelers, American coots, great blue herons, egrets, sandhill cranes, and red-winged and Brewer's blackbirds. Forest birds include flickers, robins, white-headed woodpeckers, mountain bluebirds, and red-breasted and pygmy nuthatches. Mule deer and elk roam here.

Viewing Information: Watch the open water areas along the main roadway. Spring and fall are best for ducks, geese, and other waterfowl. During summer look for pied-billed and western grebes, pelicans, ospreys, and sandhill cranes. Take the gravel road through ponderosa pine forest to Wocus Bay. In the forest, watch for elk and yellow-pine chipmunks. Mule deer can be seen browsing in meadow areas surrounding the marsh during evening and morning hours. Winter months are good times to observe bald eagles and hawk species.

Directions: From Klamath Falls, drive north 45 miles on U.S. Highway 97 and turn east on Silver Lake Road. Follow Silver Lake Road for 7 miles to refuge boundary. The road to Wocus Bay is 4.3 miles further, at the east end of the refuge.

Ownership: USFWS (503) 783-3380
Size: 37,600 acres   **Closest Town:** Chemult

Description: Upper Klamath National Wildlife Refuge contains extensive cattail and bulrush marshes. Access is by canoe or boat from Rocky Point Resort. Lower Klamath is a mix of marsh, temporary wetlands, grasslands, and agricultural lands. The majority of Pacific Flyway waterfowl passes through Lower Klamath National Wildlife Refuge, and bald eagles winter here. Self-guided driving tours along the refuge's extensive road system provide excellent access.

Viewing Information: March through May and August and September are best times for viewing. Pintails, mallards, ruddy ducks, northern shovelers, three species of heron, two species of egrets, three species of terns, sandhill cranes, white-faced ibis, American avocets, double-crested cormorants, American white pelicans, and black-necked stilts are just a few of the birds to be seen in spring, fall, and summer. Fall is a prime time to view Canada, snow, and white-fronted geese. Duck and geese populations are at their highest in early November. Large numbers of bald eagles spend the winter in and around Lower Klamath National Wildlife Refuge. November through February is best for seeing eagles, with peak numbers in mid-February.

Directions: *To reach Upper Klamath National Wildlife Refuge, take Oregon Highway 140 west from Klamath Falls 25 miles to Rocky Point Road. Follow signs for 3 miles to Rocky Point Resort. To reach Lower Klamath National Wildlife Refuge drive south from Klamath Falls 19 miles on U.S. Highway 97. At the California border turn east on California Highway 161. Refuge headquarters is 4 miles south on Hill Road off California 161.*

Ownership: USFWS (916) 667-2231
Size: 14,900 acres; 53,600 acres   **Closest Towns:** Klamath Falls, Tule Lake

The Lower Klamath National Wildlife Refuge was established by President Theodore Roosevelt in 1908 as the nation's first waterfowl refuge. Most of the migrating waterfowl of the Pacific Flyway pass through this area on their annual journeys.

GARY BRAASCH

57 EAGLE RIDGE PARK

Description: Located on a forested peninsula extending into Upper Klamath Lake, this park provides access to waterfowl-rich Shoalwater Bay. Pine and firs blanket the steep slopes above the bay, while marshland and willows line the shore. The Klamath basin is an important oasis for Canada geese, American white pelicans, terns, grebes, and numerous ducks. A well-marked trail from Kovich Grove leads along Shoalwater Bay, with spectacular views of the Cascade Mountains.

Viewing Information: Spring, summer, and fall are good times to visit. Park at the campground and walk either way along the road, scanning the lake's edge and open water for Canada geese, mallard, American white pelican, great blue heron, and Forster's tern. Western grebes can often be seen plying the waters near shore and will sometimes approach a quiet observer. Bald eagles nest along the lake. Watch for black-billed magpie, western tanager, and robin along the forest edge. Turkey vultures may be seen soaring above the trees.

Directions: *About 10 miles west of Klamath Falls on Oregon Highway 140, turn east on gravel Eagle Ridge Road. Follow signs 4 miles to park. Kovich Grove is about halfway between Oregon 140 and the park.*

Ownership: Klamath County Parks (503) 883-4696
Size: 640 acres   **Closest Town:** Klamath Falls

The only woodpecker with a white head, this medium-sized bird feeds on the seeds of sugar and ponderosa pines, as well as insects and their larvae. Found primarily in mountain areas east of the Cascades, the white-headed woodpecker depends on dead trees in old-growth forests for nesting sites.

ART WOLFE

Description: Beavers have dammed Whiskey Springs, creating extensive wetlands. Beavers are highly active here and signs of their handiwork are everywhere. These wetlands also provide habitat for waterfowl, wading birds, amphibians, and fish. Birds of interest include the wood duck, great blue heron, and sandhill crane, mallard, common yellowthroat, and yellow warbler.

Viewing Information: From the campground or day use area, hike the one-mile loop trail around the wetlands. View the wetlands from the boardwalk and observation structure. Although beavers, like most mammals, are shy and secretive, patient viewers may be rewarded by quietly watching open water at dusk. Look for the distinctive v-shape wake on the water and a dark head protruding above the surface. If a beaver startles and dives, wait a bit and it may surface again nearby. Watch for ducks, herons, and sandhill cranes during morning and evening hours. Western tree frogs may also be seen.

Directions: *From Medford, drive 30 miles east on Oregon Highway 140 to Forest Road 37 (Butte Falls/Fish Lake Road). Travel north 8 miles toward Willow Lake. Turn east on Forest Road 3065 for 0.5 mile to Whiskey Springs Campground. Trailheads to springs are located in campground and day use area.*

Ownership: USFS (503) 865-3581
Size: 30 acres   **Closest Town:** White City

Oregon's state animal, the beaver is known as a "keystone species," one that creates habitat for many other animals. Beaver dams on rivers and streams create ponds and marsh areas, providing cover and food for mink, raccoons, reptiles and amphibians, and fish.

TOM & PAT LEESON

59 ▌ LINK RIVER NATURE TRAIL

Description: This easy 1.5-mile trail follows the west bank of the willow-lined Link River. Numerous waterfowl, shorebirds, songbirds, and aquatic mammals can be found here. Watch for cliff, barn, bank, rough-winged, and tree swallows. Waterfowl includes western grebe, mallard, ruddy duck, common merganser, and double-crested cormorant. Also look for great blue and black-crowned night heron, American white pelican, Bullock's oriole, yellow-headed blackbird, Brewer's blackbird, rufous-sided towhee, scrub jay, yellow warbler, and bushtit. Mammals to watch for include mule deer, muskrat, and beaver. Two blinds along the trail offer good viewing.

Viewing Information: Spring and summer are the best times to visit. Cliff swallows nest under the Nevada Street bridge. Red-winged blackbirds are common in the willows. Grebes, pelicans, mallards, mergansers, and cormorants can be seen on the open water. Great blue herons stalk fish in shallow pools. Look for black-crowned night herons sitting on branches along the river, on the dam, or flying overhead. Red-tailed hawks often perch on power poles. Western pond turtles may be seen sunning on the log boom above the dam. Look for mammals at dawn and dusk.

Directions: *In Klamath Falls, take the Oregon Avenue/Lakeshore Drive exit from U.S. Highway 97. Turn right at bottom of exit onto Nevada Drive. Drive 0.5 mile. Parking area and trailhead are on the left immediately across the bridge. Watch for wildlife viewing signs.*

Ownership: Pacific Power and Light Company (503) 882-3411
Size: 23 acres   **Closest Town:** Klamath Falls

The marshlands and lakes of southeastern Oregon provide some of the best viewing of American white pelicans. They gather in flocks on lakes and streams, scooping up fish in their enormous bills as they swim. In spring, these birds nest on the ground in colonies.
JOE MCDONALD

Description: One of the few natural freshwater lakes in this part of the state, Dog Lake's habitats encompass marshland, moist and dry meadows, sagebrush flats, juniper and mountain mahogany woodlands, and forests of ponderosa pine and other conifers. Bald eagles, osprey, prairie falcons, turkey vultures, wild turkeys, sandhill cranes, American white pelicans, cormorants, Canada geese, western and pied-billed grebes, Forster's terns, and a variety of duck species may be seen here.

Viewing Information: Spring, summer, and fall all provide good viewing. Watch for bald eagles and osprey soaring above the lake, or perched in nearby trees. Grebes, pelicans, cormorants, and ducks are often seen plying the open waters of the lake. Look for sandhill cranes, green-winged and cinnamon teal, and other waterfowl in marshy areas. Canada geese and sandhill cranes may also be seen in open meadows. Wild turkeys keep to forested areas.

Directions: *From Lakeview, drive 6.5 miles west on Oregon Highway 140. Turn south onto County Road 1-13. Continue 4 miles and turn west onto County Road 1-11, then travel approximately 12 miles to Dog Lake.*

Ownership: USFS (503) 947-3334
Size: 5,000 acres   **Closest Town:** Lakeview

Expert swimmers and divers, the gregarious western grebe may be seen in abundance in some areas. After performing elaborate courtship rituals, pairs of grebes nest colonially in the reeds and rushes along lakes and other freshwater wetlands. They are poor fliers and must "run" along the surface of the water in order to become airborne.

LEONARD LEE RUE III

REGION 5: GREAT BASIN and OWYHEE UPLANDS

Endless sagebrush flats, barren mountain ranges and the illusion of lifelessness are often the traveler's impressions of this region. But life is abundant here. Small mammals and reptiles live among the boulders, jumbled against stark rimrock. Lakes and marshes attract huge numbers of waterfowl and other birds, for nesting, staging and resting grounds for their fall migrations south. And the careful watcher will sooner or later see fleet-footed antelope in the distance, the perfect symbol of this vast land of distant horizons.

Photo, opposite page: Buena Vista Overlook, Malhuer National Wildlife Refuge. **FRED PFLUGHOFT**

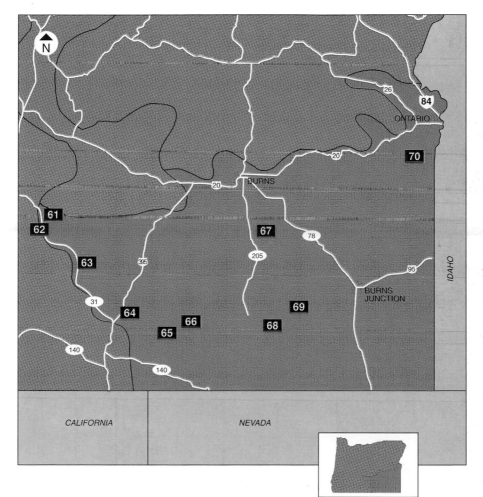

Wildlife Viewing Sites

61 Fort Rock State Park
62 Oatman Flat Deer Viewing Area
63 Summer Lake Wildlife Area
64 Lake Abert and Abert Rim
65 Warner Wetlands
66 Hart Mountain National Antelope
    Refuge
67 Malheur National Wildlife Refuge
68 Steens Mountain Loop Road
69 Mann Lake
70 Lower Owyhee River Canyon

61 FORT ROCK STATE PARK

Description: Fort Rock is all that remains of an ancient volcano. Its steep walls rise 200 feet above the sagebrush plains. This combination of habitat provides a haven for a variety of birds, particularly raptors. Look for golden eagle, red-tailed hawk, and prairie falcon. Songbirds and upland birds are also abundant. Horned lark, sage sparrow, sage thrasher, Say's phoebe, and Townsend's solitaire are seen throughout the area.

Viewing Information: Early spring through summer is the best time to visit. From the parking lot, walk along the jeep road that leads into the caldera. Scan the cliffs and sky above for golden eagle, red-tailed hawk, prairie falcon, rock dove, and raven. Great horned owls are sometimes found roosting in rock crevices and hidden ledges. Flocks of violet-green and cliff swallows may also be observed swooping along the cliffs. Watch for rock and canyon wrens along the base of the cliffs.

Directions: Just south of La Pine, take Oregon Highway 31 south for 29 miles. Turn west at the sign for Fort Rock. Follow signs for about 7.5 miles, through the town of Fort Rock, to the park.

Ownership: OPRD (503) 388-6055
Size: 190 acres   **Closest Town:** Fort Rock

62 OATMAN FLAT DEER VIEWING AREA

Description: Large herds of mule deer gather on this roadside alfalfa field surrounded by low hills of sagebrush and juniper. Pull into the roadside turnout for viewing. This site is located on private land—view from turnout only.

Viewing Information: Mule deer congregate in herds of 500 to 1,000 from November through April. Morning and evenings are best times for viewing. Bald eagles are occasionally seen here during winter.

Directions: This site is 39 miles south of La Pine, or 8 miles north of Silver Lake, on the west side of Oregon Highway 31. Watch for wildlife viewing signs.

Ownership: PVT (503) 943-3152 (ODFW)
Size: 110 acres   **Closest Town:** Silver Lake

Description: Sedge and cattail marsh, canals, and a desert lake provide an important nesting and migratory rest area for a variety of birds. The area is home to trumpeter swans and nesting snowy plovers. As many as 250 species of birds are seen here, including gadwall, redhead, Canada geese, lesser snow geese, greater white-fronted geese, American wigeon, green-winged and cinnamon teal, killdeer, American avocet, black-necked stilt, sandhill crane, great blue heron, black-crowned night heron, long-billed curlew, American white pelican, tundra swan, American coot, and snowy egret. Also look for marsh wren, savannah and song sparrow, and northern harrier. Area mammals include mule deer, coyote, and muskrat. An 8.7-mile wildlife loop, on good gravel roads, takes visitors through the area's wetlands habitat. The loop road is closed from early October through mid-January.

Viewing Information: Slowly driving the wildlife loop will yield the most sightings. Spring is the best time of year to observe migrating waterfowl and shorebirds—particularly tundra swans and snow geese. High concentrations of breeding waterfowl, wading birds, and shorebirds are seen during summer.

Directions: *Located 1.3 miles south of Summer Lake on Oregon Highway 31. Watch for wildlife viewing signs. Summer Lake is 68 miles south of La Pine and 75 miles north of Lakeview.*

Ownership: ODFW (503) 943-3152
Size: 18,000 acres   **Closest Town:** Summer Lake

Loss of habitat in its U.S. nesting grounds, due to commercial and agricultural development, nearly resulted in the trumpeter swan's extinction by the 1930s. The Oregon Department of Fish and Wildlife has been reintroducing these magnificent birds to their former range.

ART WOLFE

64 LAKE ABERT AND ABERT RIM

Description: Eighteen miles long and 10 miles wide, Lake Abert is the third largest saline body of water in North America. Rolling sagebrush-covered hills border the lake to the west, and Abert Rim towers 2,000 feet above the lake's eastern shore. The lake harbors millions of brine shrimp, an abundant food supply for waterfowl and shorebirds that nest here or pause on their spring and fall migrations. The lake supports one of the largest breeding populations of western snowy plovers in the world. Long-billed curlews and greater sandhill cranes nest in lakeside meadows. Also watch for peregrine falcons. Two herds of bighorn sheep have been established here. The Oregon lakes tui chub—a small fish—is found only in this basin. *DUE TO HIGH ALKALINITY, IT IS HAZARDOUS TO SWIM IN LAKE.*

Viewing Information: Drive the highway bordering the lake and view from numerous turnouts. Spring and fall are the best times to view eared grebes, Wilson's and red-necked phalarope, American avocet, white-faced ibis, black tern, and northern shoveler. Look for the tui chub around freshwater springs that flow into the lake. Scan the ledges and outcroppings of Abert rim with binoculars for bighorn sheep. During winter months, watch for white-tailed jackrabbits in the uplands. Watch for raptors, such as ferruginous hawk, soaring above the lake.

Directions: *From Lakeview, drive 17.4 miles north on U.S. Highway 395 to Valley Falls. Continue north 3 miles on U.S. 395. The highway parallels the lake for the next 18 miles. Interpretive information and restrooms are available on U.S. 395, located 5.6 miles north of Valley Falls.*

Ownership: BLM (503) 947-2177
Size: 100,000 acres   **Closest Town:** Valley Falls

Elusive denizens of rugged mountain slopes and rimrock, bighorn sheep are rarely seen at close range. Adult rams form separate herds during the summer months, but rejoin ewes, lambs, and young rams for the winter. The loud crack of rams butting heads during their annual fall rutting ritual can be heard up to a mile away.

LEN RUE JR.

Description: A series of interconnected lakes, potholes, marshes, and wet meadows stretches through the Warner Valley against the backdrop of Hart Mountain, providing critical habitat for nesting and migrating waterfowl, shorebirds, songbirds, and other wildlife. Residents include long-billed curlew, willet, northern shoveler, western grebe, white-faced ibis, canvasback, cinnamon teal, tundra swan, American avocet, and red-winged blackbird. Mule deer are common. The area experiences one- to three-year dry cycles, but during wet periods more than 400 miles of shoreline habitat is created. The Warner sucker is found nowhere else in the world. Restrooms and visitor information are available 2.8 miles from Plush upon entering the area. From there, gravel and dirt roads travel the length of the valley, parallel to the wetlands and lakes. *CALL AHEAD FOR CURRENT ROAD CONDITIONS AND ROUTE ADVICE. STAY ON ESTABLISHED ROADS AND WATCH FOR WET AND MUDDY CONDITIONS.*

Viewing Information: Nesting season, from April through July, and fall migration in September and October, are the best times to visit. Look for waterfowl, wading birds, and deer in marshes and wet meadows. Look for tundra swans during fall.

Directions: From Lakeview, travel north 6 miles on U.S. Highway 395 to Oregon Highway 140. Drive east 29 miles on Oregon 140. Turn north on County Road 310 and drive 18 miles to Plush. Two miles past Plush turn right on County Road 312. Visitor facilities are another 2.8 miles, on the north side of Hart Lake.

Ownership: BLM, DSL, Pvt (503) 947-2177
Size: 50,000 acres   **Closest Town:** Plush

A common bird of marshes, mudflats, and ponds, the American avocet may often be seen wading in the shallows. It catches crustaceans and insects by sweeping its thin, upturned bill with a side-to-side motion through the water.

ART WOLFE

66 HART MOUNTAIN NATIONAL ANTELOPE REFUGE

Description: Established to provide spring, summer, and fall range for prong-horn antelope, this refuge is a massive fault block ridge, which rises sharply some 3,600 feet above Warner Valley and then slopes eastward into rolling sagebrush and grassland. Highest elevation on the refuge is 8,065 feet. Numerous rugged canyons slice the escarpment's east face. Lush groves of aspen grow along the many streams and springs, while open rangeland sprawls to the horizon. Juniper uplands, stands of pine, alkaline lakes, and grassy spring-fed meadows also dot the refuge. Over 260 species of birds have been recorded here, including the endangered bald eagle and peregrine falcon. Other residents include bighorn sheep, mule deer, coyote, black-tailed jackrabbit, and ground squirrel. Refuge streams contain redband and Lahontan cutthroat trout. Visitors can relax in hot springs located at the campground. Most roads are well-maintained gravel; some are closed seasonally to protect wildlife.

Viewing Information: An early morning drive along refuge roads often yields a variety of wildlife. Spring, summer, and fall are the best seasons for seeing pronghorn. Best opportunities are in the vicinity of refuge headquarters, from Lookout Point along the Blue Sky Road, and along the road between Blue Sky and the south refuge boundary. Large concentrations of pronghorn can be found in the Spanish Flats off of the South Boundary Road during summer and fall. A high-clearance, four-wheel-drive vehicle is required to reach this area. Bighorn sheep are seen year-round along the east face of the mountain from the road between Plush and refuge headquarters. Poker Jim Ridge is also a good place to look. Hike into these areas for even better viewing opportunities. Mule deer favor the aspen and juniper groves. Walk along the aspen-lined streams at Hot Springs Campground to see common flicker, Bullock's oriole, robin, red-breasted nuthatch, wrens, yellow-bellied sapsucker, and various warblers. Sage grouse gather around refuge headquarters during early evening and at sunrise between July and October. Golden eagle, red-tailed hawk, and Swainson's hawk are often seen soaring overhead.

Directions: *Drive north from Lakeview 6 miles on U.S. Highway 395, then travel east on Oregon Highway 140 for 29 miles. Turn onto County Road 310 for 18 miles to Plush. Refuge is 27 miles from Plush. Stay on paved County Road 312 until it turns to gravel. Travel on gravel road for 9 miles up steep grade to refuge headquarters.*

Ownership: USFWS (503) 947-3315
Size: 275,000 acres   **Closest Town:** Plush

Description: This desert oasis is a major stopover and breeding area for numerous migratory birds. Two large lakes, a river, numerous small ponds, marshes, and wet meadows provide habitat for 300 species of birds and 58 species of mammals. Birds that nest on the refuge include the trumpeter swan, white-faced ibis, red-winged blackbirds, cinnamon teal, American coot, and great horned owl, as well as many other species of waterfowl, shorebirds, and songbirds. Dry, upland portions of the refuge harbor pronghorn, sage grouse, and quail. Much of the refuge is closed to hiking during the waterfowl nesting season, but extensive gravel roads provide excellent access for viewing.

Viewing Information: Spring is the best time to visit, with the arrival of migrating birds peaking in May and June. Spring migration of sandhill cranes and snow geese peaks in late March and early April. Trumpeter swans nest throughout the refuge. Look for sandhill cranes and Canada geese in open fields. Fall songbird migration peaks in late August. Refuge headquarters, the P Ranch, and Page Springs are best sites for seeing songbirds. Large numbers of waterfowl pause on Malheur Lake in September and October in preparation for their migration south. Large mule deer bucks are readily seen throughout the refuge from July through November. Look for bald eagles around the P Ranch during winter, with their numbers peaking in early March.

Directions: *From Burns, go east on Oregon Highway 78, then south on Oregon Highway 205 to milepost 25. Refuge headquarters is 9 miles east on a county road.*

Ownership: USFWS (503) 493-2612
Size: 185,000 acres   **Closest Town:** Burns

Nesting in marshlands, the sandhill crane's mating ritual involves dance-like hops and flapping wings. Migrating cranes may fly at such high altitudes that they are invisible to the naked eye. Large numbers of these birds congregate at Malheur National Wildlife Refuge from late September through October.

JOE MCDONALD

OREGON BIODIVERSITY:
FROM THE TROPICS TO THE DESERT

Neotropical migratory birds are international travelers, nesting in North America and spending the winter in Central and South America. Their annual migrations cover thousands of miles. Over 120 species of familiar Oregon birds are classified as neotropical migrants.

Ensuring the survival of neotropical migrants is a difficult task, because both their winter and summer homes must be protected. Populations of some songbirds have been in steady decline in recent years, largely due to habitat loss in both hemispheres.

Neotropical migrants such as the yellow warbler nest in dense vegetation along streams—areas particularly vulnerable to damage by human activity. But protecting habitat in Oregon will do no good if their southern wintering grounds are lost to deforestation.

68 STEENS MOUNTAIN LOOP ROAD

Description: Rising 9,700 feet above sea level, Steens Mountain is the highest peak in the northern Great Basin desert. Laced with rugged canyons, streams and springs, lush groves of aspen, high-elevation lakes, mountain meadows, and rolling sagelands, the region is rich in wildlife. Bighorn sheep, Rocky Mountain elk, mule deer, birds of prey, and a variety of songbirds are just a sampling of the mountain's residents. A 66-mile road loops through the area's most spectacular sections. *THE ROAD IS CLOSED DURING WINTER AND DOES NOT USUALLY OPEN UNTIL MID-JULY. CALL AHEAD FOR CURRENT ROAD AND WEATHER CONDITIONS.*

Viewing Information: Early mornings and evenings are best for wildlife viewing. Good viewing of elk and deer is available at Kiger Gorge Overlook from July through October. Scan the surrounding hillsides with binoculars. The prairie falcon, red-tailed hawk, American kestrel, and golden eagle can sometimes be seen here from mid-morning to late afternoon as they ride warm air currents above the gorge. For bighorn sheep, try East Rim Overlook. Look for sheep on ledges at the base of rimrock cliffs, where they seek shelter during the heat of the day. July to October is the best season for viewing bighorn sheep.

Directions: *From Burns, drive south 60 miles on Oregon Highway 205 to Frenchglen. From there, follow signs to Steens Mountain Loop Road. To reach Kiger Gorge Overlook, take the Steens Mountain North Loop Road for 22 miles. East Rim Overlook is located at the 25-mile mark.*

Ownership: BLM (503) 573-5241
Size: 200,000 acres   **Closest Town:** Frenchglen

Steens Mountain is about 20 miles long and 9,733 feet in elevation at its highest point. Glaciers have cut huge, U-shaped valleys into the mountain, some of which are accessible from the Steens Mountain Loop Road. Due to heavy winter snows, the entire loop road usually does not open until mid-July. LARRY GEDDIS

69 MANN LAKE

Description: This shallow lake surrounded by rolling sagebrush and high-desert hills provides excellent viewing opportunities for pronghorn and mule deer. Birds attracted to the lake include mallard, cinnamon teal, pintail, northern shoveler, ruddy duck, American avocet, and willet.

Viewing Information: April through October is the best time for viewing waterfowl around the lake. Deer and antelope winter here. Look for them around the lake and surrounding rangelands from December through April.

Directions: From Burns, drive east on Oregon Highway 78 to milepost 65. Turn south onto Fields/Folly Farm Road. Go 20 miles. Lake is on west side of road.

Ownership: BLM (503) 573-5241
Size: 400 acres   **Closest Town:** Fields

70 LOWER OWYHEE RIVER CANYON

Description: Rich vegetation along the river and arid sagebrush-grasslands within a high-walled canyon provide refuge and habitat for a diversity of wildlife. Mammals include mule deer, beaver, coyote, bobcat, and black-tailed jackrabbit. Birds to watch for are golden eagle, Canada geese, belted kingfisher, western kingbird, northern oriole, and rock wren. Nearby Succor Creek and Lake Owyhee State parks also provide excellent viewing.

Viewing Information: Drive the 12.5-mile paved Lake Owyhee Road to Lake Owyhee State Park. Viewing sites are marked by binocular signs. Spring and early summer are best for songbirds, fall and winter for waterfowl. Fall is best for viewing deer. Driving conditions make winter viewing difficult.

Directions: From Nyssa, drive 7.5 miles south on Oregon Highway 201 to Owyhee Junction. From Owyhee Junction, follow signs southwest to Lake Owyhee State Park. The wildlife viewing route begins in 9 miles. To reach Succor Creek State Park go south on Oregon 201 to Adrian. Continue 8 miles and turn right on gravel road, following signs 16 miles to park.

Ownership: BLM (503) 473-3144
Size: NA   **Closest Town:** Adrian

REGION 6: COLUMBIA BASIN and HIGH LAVA PLAINS

Extinct volcanoes, lava buttes, cinder cones, deep river canyons, sagebrush and scrublands, rolling grasslands, and extensive juniper forest make up this area, which stretches from the Columbia River to the center of the state. Although portions of this region have been converted to agriculture, many areas along the Columbia River remain a mecca for waterfowl and other freshwater-loving wildlife, while hawks and eagles soar over broad expanses of open country.

Photo, opposite page: Lower John Day River. **JIM YUSKAVITCH**

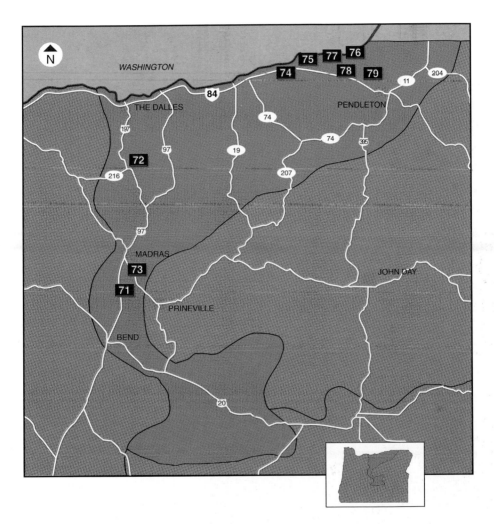

Wildlife Viewing Sites

71	Smith Rock State Park
72	Oak Springs Fish Hatchery
73	Rimrock Springs Wildlife Area
74	Well Spring
75	Irrigon Wildlife Area
76	McNary Wildlife Nature Area
77	Umatilla National Wildlife Refuge
78	Power City Wildlife Area
79	Cold Springs National Wildlife Refuge

71 SMITH ROCK STATE PARK

Description: Sheer cliffs rise up to 400 feet above the Crooked River in this desert canyon park. Internationally-renowned for rock climbing, this lush river canyon and rocky crags also provide a variety of opportunities for wildlife watching. Look for golden eagle, prairie falcon, red-tailed and rough-legged hawk, and turkey vulture. Other birds include rock dove, canyon wren, common merganser, violet green swallow, and swifts. Also watch for mule deer, porcupine, and beaver. Two miles of trails lead visitors through the canyon.

Viewing Information: Hawks and eagles nest on canyon wall ledges from April through June; scan the skies above the canyon ridges and rimrock where they soar on rising air currents. An occasional bald eagle is seen during winter months. Look for canyon wrens among the boulders and crevices at the base of cliffs. Mergansers can be seen flying up and down the river. At dusk the air is filled with flocks of violet-green swallows and swifts. Mule deer feed in the thickets and meadows along the river and in rim-top fields during the evenings. They are best viewed from the roadside, camping area, and rim overlooks. Walk quietly along the river to see beaver plying the waters or a porcupine waddling through the sagebrush and juniper.

Directions: *From Redmond, drive 4 miles north on U.S. Highway 97 to Terrebonne. Turn east on B Avenue which becomes Smith Rock Way. Drive 0.5 mile and turn left on NE 1st. Continue 2 miles and turn left onto NE 25th. Go 0.6 mile to park.*

Ownership: OPRD (503) 548-7501
Size: 641 acres   **Closest Town:** Terrebonne

Mule deer range throughout the forests and open country of eastern Oregon. As they gather together their harems in October and November, the antlered bucks may be seen sparring in non-lethal dominance combat. The mule deer's large ears are responsible for its common name. When alarmed, they bound off with a stiff-legged, hopping gait, known as "stotting."
LEN RUE JR.

Description: Springs flowing out of steep canyon walls along the Deschutes River have created a lush micro-habitat of white oak, cottonwood, alder, and blackberry thickets in an otherwise dry, sagebrush environment. Black-tailed deer, skunk, raccoon, mink, and otter live in the river canyon. Red-tailed hawk, bald eagle, and screech owl hunt here. Also look for Bullock's oriole, cedar waxwing, western tanager, black-capped chickadee, song sparrow, and western kingbird. Great blue heron and belted kingfisher ply the shallows for fish. The springs are one of the few places east of the Cascade Mountains that harbor Pacific giant salamanders. *THE GRAVEL ROAD INTO THE CANYON IS STEEP. A FOUR-WHEEL-DRIVE VEHICLE IS HIGHLY RECOMMENDED DURING WINTER MONTHS. CANYON IS HOME TO RATTLESNAKES—USE CAUTION WALKING IN WARM WEATHER.*

Viewing Information: May and June are the best months for seeing songbirds. Explore the hatchery grounds in early morning or at dusk. Birds are common among the numerous fruit trees. Also drive to the end of the road, just downstream from the hatchery. Park just before the railroad tracks and scan the dense vegetation on the uphill slope and along the wet river margins for songbirds. Mule deer sometimes travel the railroad corridor. Fish spawning at the hatchery in October. Bald eagles are easily seen roosting in trees along the tracks from December through February, with numbers peaking in January.

Directions: *From Maupin, drive 6 miles north on U.S. Highway 197. Turn east at sign for fish hatchery. Follow road 3 miles to hatchery.*

Ownership: ODFW (503) 395-2546
Size: 203 acres   **Closest Town:** Maupin

An aquatic member of the weasel family, mink prowl marshes, lakes, ponds, and rivers in search of muskrats, their preferred prey. Excellent swimmers, they also catch fish, turtles, crayfish, and frogs, as well as rabbits, snakes, and birds. Always on the move, mink are primarily nocturnal, although they are occasionally seen during the day.
ALAN & SANDY CAREY

73 RIMROCK SPRINGS WILDLIFE AREA

Description: This area offers a range of diverse wildlife habitats ,including open water, marsh, meadows, riparian areas, rocky slopes, and sagebrush and juniper uplands. A 1.5-mile trail and two observation decks provide outstanding viewing opportunities. Songbirds found here include meadowlark, mountain bluebird, Townsend's solitaire, and red-winged, Brewer's, and yellow-headed blackbird. Mallard, green-winged and cinnamon teal, Canada geese, American coot, ring-necked duck, snipe, killdeer, and great blue heron are a few of the shorebirds and waterfowl that may be seen. Raptors include golden eagle, red-tailed hawk, northern harrier, American kestrel, and great horned owl. Also watch for mule deer, pronghorn, coyote, beaver, porcupine, black-tailed jackrabbit, cottontail rabbit, and yellow-pine chipmunk.

Viewing Information: Spring and summer is best for nesting waterfowl and shorebirds. Fall and winter are prime times for viewing migrating waterfowl as well as for hawks and eagles. Spring and fall are peak times for songbirds.

Directions: Adjacent to U.S. Highway 26, 10 miles south of Madras, on the Crooked River National Grassland.

Ownership: USFS (503) 447-9640, 447-5111 (ODFW)
Size: 430 Acres   **Closest Town:** Madras

74 WELL SPRING

Description: This area of remnant native grasslands and shrublands supports such birds as the burrowing owl, ferruginous and Swainson's hawk, golden eagle, horned lark, nighthawk, and grasshopper sparrow. One of the world's largest populations of long-billed curlews nests here. Also watch for Washington ground squirrel, mule deer, bobcat, badger, coyote, and black-tailed jackrabbit. The Oregon Trail passed through this site. Old wagon ruts, remains of a stagecoach station, and an emigrant cemetery can be found in the area.

Viewing Information: Spring and summer are the best times to visit. Look for raptors aloft on afternoon air currents. Mammals are less visible; best chances for viewing are at dawn and dusk.

Directions: From Boardman, travel east on Interstate 84. Take Exit 168. Drive south about 17 miles on U.S. Highway 730 to Juniper Road. Turn right, then go right again onto Immigrant Road. Follow Immigrant Road and signs to site.

Ownership: DOD (206) 481-2565
Size: 80 acres   **Closest Town:** Boardman

75 IRRIGON WILDLIFE AREA

Description: This wildlife area lies along an eight-mile stretch of the Columbia River and includes riparian and desert habitat and 44 ponds. Painted turtles and long-billed curlews are two wildlife highlights of the area. Mule deer and black-tailed jackrabbits live here. The area also provides good habitat for Canada geese, mallard, merganser, great blue heron, barn and violet-green swallow, and numerous species of warbler, finch, and sparrow.

Viewing Information: Spring is the ideal time to visit. Look for curlews, herons, ducks, and other waterfowl around ponds and along the river. Scan ponds for painted turtles sunning on logs and rocks. Jackrabbits are most likely seen in desert scrub. Mule deer may be seen throughout the area; early morning and evenings are best. Flocks of swallows swoop over ponds at dusk as they feed on insects. Look for warblers in thickets along the river and ponds.

Directions: *The area borders the Columbia north of U.S. Highway 730 between Irrigon and Umatilla city limits. Best access is by foot from Irrigon Park in Irrigon.*

Ownership: ACE (503) 276-2344 (ODFW)
Size: 940 acres   **Closest Town:** Irrigon

76 MCNARY WILDLIFE NATURE AREA

Description: This desert, steppe, and wetlands ecosystem along the Columbia River harbors a variety of wildlife. Ponds, meandering streams, and marshes provide habitat for mule deer and beaver, and also frogs and turtles. Waterfowl and wading birds include great blue heron, black-crowned night heron, tundra swan, mallard, wood duck, and cinnamon teal. Also look for osprey, northern harrier, and bank swallow. Upland species to watch for are ring-necked pheasant, California quail, red-tailed hawk, American kestrel, and robin. Black-tailed jackrabbits are common. Canoeing is permitted on ponds and streams.

Viewing Information: Fall and spring migration periods are best for seeing songbirds. Ducks, geese, and other waterfowl are present year-round, but fall and spring offer the best viewing. Look for bald eagles from November until March in cottonwood trees along Columbia River. Frog Pond 2 and Social Security Pond are good places to see tundra swans from November through January. Look for mule deer early in the day during winter, north of Third Street between Ferry Road and Bridge Road.

Directions: *From Umatilla, go east 0.5 mile on U.S. Highway 730. Turn north into McNary Dam main entrance. Follow road to bottom of dam. Go west on 3rd Street, following signs to nature area.*

Ownership: ACE (503) 922-4388
Size: 500 acres   **Closest Town:** Umatilla

77 | UMATILLA NATIONAL WILDLIFE REFUGE

Description: Native shrub-steppe desert, wet woodlands, and cattail and bulrush marsh characterize this refuge, where waterfowl in the hundreds of thousands gather during the fall migration. Look for mallard, Canada geese, blue-winged and cinnamon teal, American white pelican, long-billed curlew, black-billed magpie, short-eared owl, burrowing owl, northern harrier, and bald eagle. Mule deer also roam here. The refuge also offers one-mile and four-mile wildlife observation trails.

Viewing Information: Waterfowl are most abundant here during fall, winter, and spring, peaking in November. Look for them in ponds and marshes. Long-billed curlews are most likely seen from March through May. Look and listen for them in desert and cropland areas. Burrowing owls are best viewed from April to June, perched on shrubs and fenceposts along roads. Bald eagle concentrations are highest in November and December; look in large trees near water. Mule deer are most commonly seen from October through January.

Directions: *From Interstate 84, take U.S. Highway 730 north for 3 miles. Continue north on Paterson Ferry Road to McCormack Unit of refuge.*

Ownership: USFWS (503) 922-3232
Size: 8,879 acres   **Closest Town:** Boardman

Dwelling in open country and nesting colonially in the abandoned burrows of mammals, burrowing owls are active both day and night. They are often seen standing by their burrows, or perched on a nearby shrub or fencepost. If disturbed in their burrow, they may give a warning call that sounds like a rattlesnake. Well Spring and the Umatilla National Wildlife Refuge are good places to search for burrowing owls.

LEN RUE JR.

78 POWER CITY WILDLIFE AREA

Description: Numerous waterfowl, upland gamebirds, shorebirds, and wading birds drawn are to these desert-encircled wetlands. Common species include mallard, teal, northern shoveler, great blue heron, ring-necked pheasant, and a variety of warblers. Hiking trails lead visitors to ponds throughout the area. Groves of Russian olive trees provide habitat for songbirds.

Viewing Information: Winter is the best time to view waterfowl. Hike the trails to ponds for waterfowl and herons. Pheasants are seen throughout the area. Spring and summer is best for seeing songbirds. Look for warblers and lazuli buntings in riparian areas and in olive tree groves.

Directions: From Hermiston, drive 2 miles north on U.S. Highway 395. Parking area is on gravel road 0.1 mile east of highway. Trails lead from parking area to ponds.

Ownership: BLM (503) 276-2344 (ODFW)
Size: 100 **Closest Town:** Hermiston

79 COLD SPRINGS NATIONAL WILDLIFE REFUGE

Description: As many as 30,000 ducks and 10,000 Canada geese converge on this desert lake during peak periods in the winter. Also look for bald and golden eagle, great blue heron, and egret. Songbirds include marsh wren, yellow-rumped warbler, western tanager, white-crowned sparrow, and American goldfinch.

Viewing Information: Winter is the best time to view Canada geese, mallard, green-winged and cinnamon teal, pintail, ruddy duck, and other waterfowl on the lake. Tundra swan and American white pelican can sometimes be seen if the lake is not frozen over. Boaters are welcome, but only paddles and electric motors are allowed. Look for songbirds during spring and fall in the southeast portion of the refuge. Numerous shorebirds are present in fall. Look for herons and egrets feeding along the water's edge.

Directions: Drive 7 miles east of Hermiston on Stanfield Loop Road.

Ownership: USFWS (503) 922-3232
Size: 3,117 acres **Closest Town:** Hermiston

REGION 7: BLUE MOUNTAINS

Six mountain ranges make up the rugged and complex topography of this region, where elevations reach to ten thousand feet above sea level. Forests of Douglas-fir and grand fir predominate, along with ponderosa pine and other conifers, sagebrush steppe, and grasslands. Herds of mule deer and Rocky Mountain elk wander the high country. Sharp-eyed viewers may be rewarded with a glimpse of bighorn sheep off on some distant mountain precipice.

Photo, opposite page: Wallowa Lake. **LARRY GEDDIS**

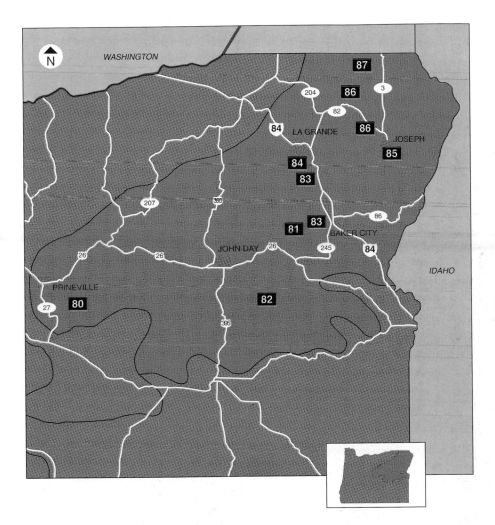

Wildlife Viewing Sites

80	Upper Crooked River Bald Eagle Viewing Tour
81	Sumpter Valley Wildlife Area
82	Logan Valley Interpretive Site
83	Elkhorn Wildlife Area
84	Ladd Marsh Wildlife Area
85	Wallowa State Park
86	Enterprise and Spring Branch Wildlife Areas
87	Wenaha Wildlife Area

80 | UPPER CROOKED RIVER BALD EAGLE VIEWING TOUR

Description: Bald eagles from as far away as Canada's Northwest Territories spend the winter in the upper Crooked River valley. Congregations of as many as 50 eagles have been seen here. The golden eagle, prairie falcon, American kestrel, northern harrier, and rough-legged and red-tailed hawk are also present. Habitat is varied, from pasture and floodplain along the river to steep rimrock. *BE PREPARED FOR COLD WEATHER AND WINTERY DRIVING CONDITIONS WHEN TRAVELING IN THIS AREA.*

Viewing Information: The viewing period runs from December through April. February through early April are best, with viewing at its peak in March. Optimum viewing occurs from 9 a.m. to 3 p.m. as the eagles move out of their nightly roosts to feed. Drive the route and watch for them soaring, in pastures, or perched in trees along the river. It is common to see 40 or more bald and golden eagles along this tour. Also watch for various species of hawks.

Directions: From Prineville, drive 1 mile east on U.S. Highway 26. Turn south onto the Paulina Highway. Drive east 25 miles to Post. Continue on the Paulina Highway following the Crooked River.

Ownership: BLM, Pvt. (503) 447-4115 (BLM)
Size: NA   **Closest Town:** Prineville

81 | SUMPTER VALLEY WILDLIFE AREA

Description: This site is on the Powder River at the Dredge Depot Recreation Area. Numerous water-filled potholes, dense thickets of willows, riparian habitat, scattered pines, and scrub provide habitat for mule deer, cottontail rabbit, ground squirrel, and beaver. Also watch for Canada geese, ring-necked ducks, and bitterns. A three-mile trail loops through the area.

Viewing Information: Hike the trail from April to July for best viewing. Ducks and geese are found along the river and in potholes near the depot. Look for red-winged blackbirds in cattails surrounding the potholes, and warblers and other songbirds in willow thickets. Cottontails also favor these brushy areas. Chipmunk and golden-mantled ground squirrel are common around depot.

Directions: From Baker City, drive 24 miles west on Oregon Highway 7. Turn left on Dredge Loop Road at the sign for Railroad Park. Park at the Sumpter Valley Dredge Depot and Museum.

Ownership: Baker County (503) 898-2826 (ODFW)
Size: 1,578 acres   **Closest Town:** Sumpter

Description: This site was once heavily used by prehistoric people. Today this mosaic of wet and dry meadows, riparian habitat, and ponderosa pine forest contains the largest population of upland sandpipers in the western U.S. Two other sensitive species, the sandhill crane and long-billed curlew, are also found here. Other residents include pronghorn and mule deer. The Strawberry Mountain Wilderness, five miles north, provides a spectacular backdrop.

Viewing Information: Spring is the best time to see upland sandpipers, sandhill cranes, and long-billed curlews. Look for them in wet meadows and marshy areas. Spring and summer is ideal for songbirds. Look for the common yellowthroat, Wilson's warbler, and yellow warbler amidst dense riparian vegetation. Mountain bluebirds are found throughout the area. Watch for red-tailed hawks soaring above. Summer and fall are prime seasons for viewing pronghorn and mule deer. Watch for them in open meadow areas during early morning and late afternoon hours. Early evening is a particularly good time to see deer.

Directions: *From U.S. Highway 26 in Prairie City, take County Road 62 south to Forest Road 16. Drive 7 miles on Forest Road 16 to the site.*

Ownership: USFS (503) 820-3311
Size: 5 acres   **Closest Town:** Prairie City

Most common at elevations above 5,000 feet, the mountain bluebird hunts insects by hovering close to the ground. The bright blue male is easily recognized. Look for them in meadows and rangelands. Logan Valley and Hart Mountain National Antelope Refuge are good places to see mountain bluebirds. ALAN & SANDY CAREY

83 ELKHORN WILDLIFE AREA

Description: This site was established to provide winter feeding range for local herds of Rocky Mountain elk, which were damaging private agricultural lands. Rolling foothill country of meadows, sagebrush rangelands, and forests of pine, larch, and juniper, provides excellent opportunities to see these magnificent animals during the appropriate season. Herds of mule deer also roam here.

Viewing Information: Foot travel is prohibited from December 1 to April 15, but viewing sites are provided along roads. Visitors should remain in vehicles to avoid disturbing elk. The area is divided into two separate tracts. Elk and deer forage on the Auburn Tract from December 1 to March 1. Look for the viewing site, marked by binocular logo sign, immediately to the left upon entering the area. Two viewing sites are available on the North Powder Tract. One is located on North Powder River Lane, the other off Tucker Flat Road. Elk gather on this tract from December 1 to April 1.

Directions: *From Interstate 84 north of Baker City, take Exit 285 at North Powder. Turn left off of exit and follow binocular signs 9 miles west on North Powder River Lane to reach North Powder Tract viewing site. To reach the Tucker Flat Road viewing site, turn right onto Tucker Flat Road upon entering the wildlife area. Go 2.3 miles, then turn right to viewing area. Follow binocular signs. To reach the Auburn Tract from Baker City, go west 7 miles on Oregon Highway 7. Turn west on Auburn Road and drive 3.3 miles to site.*

Ownership: ODFW (503) 898-2826
Size: 7,772 acres   **Closest Town:** Baker City

No sound is more evocative of the western mountain wilderness than the "bugle," or call of a bull elk on an October morning. During the autumn rut, bulls may amass a harem of up to 60 cows. A bull elk's haunting call lets the cows know who is boss, and serves as an invitation to any other bull who cares to challenge him for dominance.

MICHAEL S. SAMPLE

84 LADD MARSH WILDLIFE AREA

Description: Established to protect migrating and nesting waterfowl, this area boasts the largest remnant native tule marsh in northeastern Oregon. Croplands, wetlands, and upland vegetation round out the habitat. White-tailed and mule deer and Rocky Mountain elk roam here. Birds to watch for include bald eagle, short-eared owl, sandhill crane, American avocet, mallard, gadwall, teal, northern shoveler, bobolink, and numerous other hawks, waterfowl, and songbirds. A nature trail, wildlife observation points, and photo blind are available. From mid-January through mid-October entry is by permit only, for educational groups. Group tours available. Call for more information.

Viewing Information: Spring and fall are best for seeing waterfowl and shorebirds. Elk and deer are most visible during winter months. View wildlife from adjacent roads, observation points, or photo blind.

Directions: *From La Grande, drive 5 miles south on Interstate 84. Take Exit 268 to Foothill Road. Turn right on Foothill Road. Go 2 miles to reach viewpoint. To reach the nature trail, turn left on Foothill Road and go 400 yards. Pierce Road and Hot Lake Lane provide additional viewing sites. Photo blind is located 7 miles east of La Grande on Oregon Highway 203.*

Ownership: ODFW (503) 963-4954
Size: 3,208 acres   **Closest Town:** La Grande

85 WALLOWA LAKE STATE PARK

Description: A glacial-carved, forest lake nestled against the spectacular Eagle Cap Wilderness is the setting for this park. Mule deer are common here and easily seen. Red squirrel, raccoon, golden-mantled ground squirrel, osprey, and bald eagle also inhabit the area.

Viewing Information: Present year-round, deer are most active mornings and evenings. The best place to view them is in the campground where they often tolerate close approach. Ground and tree squirrels can also be seen in the campground. In summer, look for osprey flying over the lake or perched in trees on shore. Bald eagles are sometimes seen in the same areas during fall.

Directions: *The park is 6 miles south of Joseph on Oregon Highway 82.*

Ownership: OPRD (503) 432-8855
Size: 166 acres   **Closest Town:** Joseph

86 ENTERPRISE AND SPRING BRANCH WILDLIFE AREAS

Description: Woodlands, wetlands, river, and riparian vegetation provide habitat for numerous species of waterfowl, songbirds, and mammals. Look for white-tailed and mule deer, beaver, mink, and muskrats. Birds found here include the marsh wren, Virginia rail, sora, and great blue heron.

Viewing Information: Late spring and early summer are best times to visit. Look for Canada geese, mallard, great blue heron, long-billed marsh wren, and red-winged blackbird in wetlands of the Enterprise Wildlife Area. Sora, rail, and snipe stay in dense grassy areas and are difficult to see. White-tailed deer also roam this area. Mule deer are found at Spring Branch Wildlife Area. Both species browse in open marshy areas at dawn and dusk. Mink, muskrat, and beaver are seen at both sites.

Directions: *To reach the Enterprise Wildlife Area, drive 2 miles west of Enterprise on Oregon Highway 82. Turn south onto Fish Hatchery Road. Area is on the left, just before the hatchery. Spring Branch Wildlife Area is on the north side of Oregon 82, 2 miles east of Wallowa where the road leaves the Wallowa River.*

Ownership: ODFW (503) 426-3279
Size: 32 acres; 8 acres   **Closest Town:** Enterprise, Wallowa

87 WENAHA WILDLIFE AREA

Description: A prime location for viewing wintering herds of mule deer, Rocky Mountain elk, and bighorn sheep. Bald eagle and wild turkey can also be seen here. *ACCESS REQUIRES A STEEP DESCENT ON GRAVEL ROAD.* Four-wheel-drive vehicles recommended during winter months.

Viewing Information: November through March are the best months for viewing. Look for elk on Eden Bench and for deer and bighorn sheep on the Eden Bench breaks. Mornings and evenings are best. Watch for eagles along the Grande Ronde River. Turkeys may be seen along the road between Troy and Eden Bench.

Directions: *From Enterprise, travel north on Oregon Highway 3 to Flora. Follow signs to Troy, 14 miles down steep gravel road. Use caution. Watch for log trucks. For a less steep access route, continue from Flora on Oregon 3. Cross over Washington border to Washington Highway 129. After crossing the Grande Ronde go left on County Road 100 for 18 miles to Troy. Area headquarters is located 1 mile north of Troy along River Road. Follow signs to Eden Bench and other Wildlife Area lands.*

Ownership: ODFW (503) 828-7721
Size: 12,300 acres   **Closest Town:** Troy

POPULAR WILDLIFE VIEWING SPECIES OF OREGON
— AND WHERE TO FIND THEM

The index below identifies some of the more interesting and readily seen wildlife in Oregon and some of the locations where they are most likely to be found. Many of the animals listed here may be viewed at other sites as well. The numbers following each listing are site numbers, not page numbers.

WHERE THE WILD THINGS ARE

Falcon Press puts wildlife viewing secrets at your fingertips with our high-quality, full color guidebooks—the Watchable Wildlife series. This is the only official series of guides for the National Watchable Wildlife Program: areas featured in the books correspond to official sites across America. And you'll find more than just wildlife. Many sites boast beautiful scenery, interpretive displays, opportunities for hiking, picnics, biking, plus—a little peace and quiet. So pick up one of our Wildlife Viewing Guides today and get close to Mother Nature!

WATCH THIS PARTNERSHIP WORK

The National Watchable Wildlife Program was formed with one goal in mind: get people actively involved in wildlife appreciation and conservation. Defenders of Wildlife has led the way by coordinating this unique multi-agency program and developing a national network of prime wildlife viewing areas.

Part of the proceeds go to conserve wildlife and wildlife habitat.
Call toll-free or write for a free catalog.
1-800-582-2665
Falcon Press, P.O. Box 1718,
Helena, Montana 59624